SIRIOUSLY
❊ DELICIOUS ❊

SIRIOUSLY
· DELICIOUS *·*

100 Nutritious (and Not So Nutritious)
Simple Recipes for the Real Home Cook

SIRI DALY

Oxmoor
House.

For my Mom, who founded my
"fan club." And for my O'Mo,
who enthusiastically joined.
Co-Grannies for life.

Editorial Director: Anja Schmidt

Project Editor: Melissa Brown

Design Director: Melissa Clark

Photo Director: Paden Reich

Senior Designer: Allison Chi

Designer: Matt Ryan

Photographers: Caitlin Bensel,
    Jennifer Causey, Kelsey Hansen,
    Alison Miksch, Victor Protasio,
    Scott Rounds

Prop Stylists: Kay E. Clarke,
    Missie Crawford, Thom Driver,
    Heather Chadduck Hillegas,
    Kashara Johnson, Karin Olsen

Food Stylists: Mary Claire Britton,
    Torie Cox, Margaret Monroe Dickey,
    Eugene Jho, Karen Rankin

Food Stylist Assistants: Will Driskill,
    Blakeslee Giles, Rishon Hanners,
    Pam Lolley, Elise Mayfield,
    Ivy Odom

Recipe Developers and Testers:
    Allene Arnold,
    Time Inc. Food Studios

Assistant Production Director:
    Sue Chodakiewicz

Senior Production Manager:
    Greg A. Amason

Copy Editor: Jacqueline Giovanelli

Proofreader: Dolores Hydock

Indexer: Mary Ann Laurens

Fellows: Kaitlyn Pacheco,
    Holly Ravazzolo, Hanna Yokeley

Hair and Makeup: Valerie Star

ISBN-13: 978-0-8487-5580-5

Signed Version
ISBN-13: 978-0-8487-5891-2

Library of Congress Control
Number: 2017961303

First Edition 2018

Printed in the United States
of America

10 9 8 7 6 5 4 3 2 1

We welcome your comments and
suggestions about Time Inc. Books.

Time Inc. Books
Attention: Book Editors
P.O. Box 62310
Tampa, Florida 33662-2310

Time Inc. Books products may be
purchased for business or promotional use.
For information on bulk purchases, please
contact Christi Crowley in the Special Sales
Department at (845) 895-9858.

contents

Kale and
Avocado Salad
with Crispy
Breadcrumbs
PG 192

Foreword

THE FIRST TIME SIRI AND CARSON invited us to their house for dinner, she was quick to tell me what the menu was going to be, even though the date was weeks away. "Does that sound ok?" she emailed. "Sorry, food is pretty much all we think about around here!"

That was my first introduction to what cooking and food and the kitchen mean to Siri. I have come to see that my sweet friend loves to dream up meals and experiment and design just the right menu—because to do so is to create a memory and connection with friends that starts in the kitchen and ends hours later, around the table, lost in laughs and conversation. To be in Siri's kitchen is to be in her warmth and her humor and her light. It's to be in her family.

And somehow, she makes it all look so effortless. For years I begged—BEGGED!—for her chocolate chip cookie recipe, the secret to her irresistible little morsels of diet ruin. But she swore to me there was no secret ingredient, no magic element. She dutifully sent along her recipe but—spoiler alert—mine did not turn out like hers. And then I finally figured it out: She is, simply, supremely talented and has mastered/invented techniques that make the cookies sweeter, the dressing tangier, the chicken juicier, the potatoes crispier, the sauce yummier, the everything...better. Whatever Siri makes, it's the best you've ever had. Turns out, SHE is the secret ingredient.

I wish everyone could sit at her kitchen counter, drinking cocktails and cracking up while she is somehow creating a meal you will never forget. But these pages are the closest thing, and I have watched as she has poured her heart and creativity and talents into the book you hold in your hands. Enjoy!!

—SAVANNAH GUTHRIE

Halloween Chef (please note the snowboots, thanks Minnesota).

↳ Child labor is fun!

Making Cookies with Grandma Etta(and pooping my diaper at the same time).

I promise we are enjoying this!

Dyeing eggs with Mama (again, we're having fun, I swear).

Introduction

THE CRAZIEST THING happened to me after my first child was born: I...became...a mother. No seriously, it's true! The nurses at the hospital handed over my son, and let me take him home...WITHOUT THEM. They said, "You are a parent now; goodbye." As much as I thought I had prepared during my pregnancy for the responsibility that parenthood requires, it soon became apparent that I had no actual clue what I was doing. So, I did what any resourceful human being would do, and I figured it out, day by day. From swaddling to nursing to sleep training...life was a series of triumphs and failures, and even after the biggest flops (like incorrectly buckling the car seat for an entire week), it all felt completely worth it.

Around the time my son started eating solid foods, I made the decision not to return to work as a Producer on my husband's late-night show, *Last Call with Carson Daly*. I was "mom-ing" hard and loving it, yet felt an ache for something more, a yearning to explore what was beyond poopy diapers, and that's when a second baby—my blog Siriously Delicious—was born. It began as a way to keep track of the food I was cooking for my little family, but over time evolved into so much more.

The decision to write about food was a no-brainer; it has always been a passion of mine. Growing up in Minnesota meant that it was winter most of the year (#seasonhog), and when you're cold and stuck indoors, you eat! More than that, though, you gather with kinfolk around a warm hearthstone and prepare comforting, soulful meals...I grew up in olden times, by the way. That act of collectively producing something for all to enjoy is the best part about food. My family shared this sentiment. During meals, we were constantly discussing what the next one would be. Our reunions, vacations, and holidays have always been focused on culinary excursions. Basically, I was raised to eat, breathe, and sleep food (or just eat it, because that's the part that makes sense).

Fast forward to later in life: I am now a mother (of three kids), a wife (to just one husband), and almost solely responsible for churning out daily meals. As any busy human knows, that grind is never easy, and inspiration can be hard to come by. In the beginning, I needed encouragement, and my blog began to provide a regular source of stimulation. I started testing out recipes, both online and in cookbooks, and eventually devising my own—documenting both the good and the bad. An audience began to materialize, and then, what felt like a community of people with the same objective: to have fun in the kitchen. Much like parenthood, cooking asks you to trust your instincts. I discovered that recipes are like blueprints: a template for your taste buds. They shouldn't intimidate, instead, they should motivate.

It all boils down (pun intended) to my philosophy for cooking, which is this: Don't take it so Siri-ously. Do you see what I did there? Puns are fun! Simply put: Cooking should be just as enjoyable as eating. The recipes in this book were developed with that in mind. They are approachable, straightforward, and of course, delicious. My goal is to create adaptable dishes (shout out to my picky eaters!). They are designed to fit into our balanced lifestyles, with quick dishes for those hectic days and more involved ones for relaxed occasions. The six chapters are organized to show how I get through my day: with breakfast, lunch, dinner, sides, happy hour (!!) and, of course, dessert. Whether you're a chef, or a self-taught cook like myself, this book is about loving food. You don't have to be aware of the newest restaurants or the hottest cooking trends to appreciate what *Siriously Delicious* represents.

So without further ado, I humbly introduce you to my first cookbook. Pinch me! I am so thankful for my family of taste testers, for my husband who allows me to photograph his food before he eats it, for the support of my friends and for YOU...for being a part of this culinary journey. Let's eat!

Wakey Wakey!

Good Morning! Rise and Shine! Wakey Wakey, Eggs and Bakey! Am I irritating you yet? The truth is, hearing any of these early morning expressions before coffee and something to eat is simply disturbing. While they are meant to motivate your day, words are not enough. Coffee. Coffee and food are enough, and then enthusiasm may follow. All of this is coming from a morning person, by the way. I truly enjoy that "crack of dawn" atmosphere…the quiet promise of a new day, a fresh start, or as my mother-in-law used to say, another chance to get it right.

Of course, the best part of mornings for me is that small window of time when my kids are still asleep, my husband is at work, and I can collect my thoughts and plans for the day...with my best friend Coffee, obviously. Then, just like that, chaos ensues. Everyone wakes up, and everyone is hungry. Enter, the most important meal of them all: breakfast, the delicious and nutritious fuel your body requires to kick-start the day. Whether you drink it, spread it on toast, scramble it up, or sprinkle it with powdered sugar, breakfast has much to offer. From the sweet to the savory, it fills our sleepy bellies and wakes up our foggy minds, preparing us to take on anything! Too much? Okay, sure, it might not always be that simple. I still have to practically spoon-feed my oldest child in the morning because he seems to constantly move in slow motion. Or I often get the "I'm not hungry" retort where I'm left shoving food down their mouths as they walk to the bus. And once they are finally in school, I will suddenly realize that my stomach is empty and I'm starving and grumpy. Like so many families, we're all eating different things at different times so I've developed a variety of recipes to make breakfast as efficient—and yummy—as possible.

This chapter has something for any palate and any circumstance, from those busy, eat-on-the-go occasions to those lazy, weekend mornings when breakfast becomes brunch. There are kid-friendly options like 5-Ingredient Peanut Butter Granola Bars and Perfect Banana Minimuffins as well as my personal favorites, like Chorizo Hash Breakfast Burritos and Egg-in-Hole Avocado Toast. You will love the nutritious options, like Tropical Green Smoothie with Fruit and Granola and Mini Frozen Fruit and Yogurt Parfaits, and you will drool over the not-so-nutritious options, like Browned Butter Caramelized Banana Bread and Dark Chocolate Croissant Bread Pudding. You guys, we live in a world where it is acceptable to eat that for breakfast! This makes me happy. Many of these recipes would even make the perfect Breakfast for Dinner, in which case I say, "Winner, Winner, Breakfast Dinner!" (I don't really say that).

No matter what mood you're in, the ingredients available to you, or the time you have to work with, you will find something you love within this chapter. Now go forth, and seize the day! (Or at the very least, pour yourself some coffee.) Cock-a-Doodle-Doo!

Tropical Green Smoothie with Fruit and Granola

3 cups loosely packed baby kale or spinach leaves

2 cups frozen pineapple chunks

2 cups unsweetened refrigerated coconut milk

1 cup fresh seedless green grapes

1 cup ice cubes

1 ½ teaspoons minced fresh ginger

1 medium-sized ripe avocado

There was a time in my life when I would have made fun of a green smoothie. Probably around the same time that I frequented tanning beds and only did laundry once a week. If you're not familiar with this time period, it's usually around 22 to 26 years of age when you don't really take care of yourself (my skin hates that twenty-something self). Now that I'm old and wise, I am ALL about a good smoothie...the greener, the better. Should we talk about why smoothies are so conveniently nutritious? Nothing is easier to whip up because all you need is a good blender. I mean it, you really can't mess them up. The flavor combinations are endless. Almost all of them are packed with vitamins, minerals, healthy proteins and antioxidants. Also, you can drink them in a glass or serve them in a shallow bowl, topped with fresh fruits, granola, seeds and shaved coconut. This particular smoothie gets its tropical sweetness from the pineapples and grapes, its creaminess from the coconut milk and avocado, and its "Why is this so good?!" from the fresh ginger. It lends the perfect punch to this perfect breakfast. Take THAT, younger self.

Combine all of the ingredients in a blender; process until smooth, stopping and scraping down the sides of the blender as needed. Divide the mixture between 2 glasses, and serve immediately.

SIRIOUSLY SIMPLE

To make for simple assembly in the mornings, combine small plastic containers of premeasured fruits and veggies in your refrigerator and your freezer, so you can just toss in the blender and go. Refrigerate: avocado, kale, grapes, and coconut milk. Freeze: pineapple chunks.

SIRIOUSLY MINI

I love to freeze green grapes for snack time because kids think they taste like mini popsicles! For the real little ones, slice them in half before freezing.

Mini Frozen Fruit and Yogurt Parfaits

SERVES **6**

HANDS-ON TIME: **20 MINUTES**

TOTAL TIME: **2 HOURS 35 MINUTES**

It's a well-known fact that my children are picky eaters. After taking a bite of an apple, my youngest daughter was once famously quoted saying, "There is too much apple in this apple." (Then she spit it out, if you must know.) Of course as they get older, their palates expand and they are less afraid of trying things, but I'm always on the lookout for fun recipes that star fruits or vegetables. Enter: these cute bite-sized frozen parfaits. You assemble everything in a mini muffin pan, starting with your favorite crunchy granola, adding creamy Greek yogurt and topping it all off with sweet pieces of fruit. Once frozen, they are the perfect on-the-go breakfast or any-time-of-day treat.

½ cup finely diced fresh strawberries

2 teaspoons granulated sugar

½ cup finely diced fresh peaches

¾ cup granola (without dried fruit)

2 cups vanilla whole-milk Greek yogurt

½ cup fresh blueberries

12 fresh raspberries

1 Place mini paper baking liners in each of the 24 cups in the miniature muffin pans. Toss together the diced strawberries and 1 teaspoon of the sugar in a small bowl. Toss together the diced peaches with the remaining 1 teaspoon sugar in a separate small bowl. Let the fruit stand in bowls until slightly juicy, about 15 minutes.

2 Meanwhile, lightly chop or crush any large pieces of granola; sprinkle about 1 teaspoon granola on the bottom of each baking liner. Set aside the remaining granola.

3 Spoon the yogurt into a ziplock plastic bag. Seal the bag, and snip 1 bottom corner to make a hole. Pipe a layer of yogurt on top of the granola in each muffin cup. Layer half of the muffin cups with diced strawberries, another layer of yogurt, and a few blueberries. Top the remaining muffin cups with diced peaches, another layer of yogurt, and 1 raspberry. Top all the muffin cups with ½ teaspoon each of the remaining granola. Cover the muffin pans with plastic wrap, and place in the freezer until frozen, about 2 hours. Store the parfaits in the freezer for up to 2 weeks.

SIRIOUSLY MINI

Get your kids involved in making these little breakfast treats. Let them choose the combinations of fruits and yogurt flavors to make it more interesting for them. They might make a mess, but that's part of the fun! (I swear.)

- **½ pound fresh Mexican chorizo, casings removed**
- **1 medium russet potato, diced**
- **1 small red onion, chopped**
- **1 small red bell pepper, chopped**
- **2 tablespoons salted butter**
- **8 large eggs**
- **½ teaspoon kosher salt**
- **½ teaspoon black pepper**
- **½ cup shredded Monterey Jack cheese**
- **4 (8-inch) flour tortillas**
- **¾ cup shredded sharp Cheddar cheese**
- **¼ cup chopped fresh cilantro**
- **Cooking spray**
- **Sour cream**
- **Avocado Pico de Gallo (page 155)**
- **Sriracha chili sauce**

SIRIOUSLY MINI

Make these with plain breakfast sausage or turkey sausage instead of chorizo for a less spicy breakfast. It's also fun to turn the burritos into quesadillas by sprinkling the cheese over the tortilla surface, topping with the vegetable hash, sausage and eggs, and folding the tortilla in half, creating a half-moon shape. Spray and brown in the skillet and cut into wedges for little fingers to pick up on the go.

Chorizo Hash Breakfast Burritos

What I miss most about living in California are the breakfast burritos (sorry, West Coast friends, West Coast family and beautiful weather, you are all close seconds). Alas, since I cannot satisfy my craving at a local joint anymore, I enjoy making them at home. Yes, this is more time-consuming than pouring a bowl of cereal, but the end result is completely worth it. When crispy, diced potatoes get together with fluffy eggs, spicy chorizo and gooey cheese, you are left with pure breakfast burrito magic. The key to this recipe is heating the assembled product at the end for a lovely, golden crisp. Not only will they be easier to eat, the texture will also be heavenly. This is a great, savory way to start your day...and the best part? They come without earthquakes! I'm a comedian.

1   Heat a large nonstick skillet over medium-high. Add the chorizo, and cook, stirring often, with a wooden spoon to crumble, until well browned, about 8 minutes. Using a slotted spoon, remove the chorizo to drain on a paper plate lined with paper towels; reserve the drippings in the skillet.

2   Add the potato to the hot drippings, and cook, stirring frequently, until almost tender, about 7 minutes. Add the onion and bell pepper, and cook, stirring occasionally, until the potatoes are tender inside, crispy on the outside, and the onion and bell pepper are tender and lightly browned, about 5 minutes. Transfer to the plate with chorizo.

3   Wipe the skillet clean, and place over medium heat. Melt the butter in the skillet. Whisk together the eggs, salt, and pepper until well blended; pour into the skillet, and sprinkle with the Monterey Jack cheese. Cook, stirring and scraping the bottom of the pan constantly, until the eggs are scrambled to the desired degree of doneness and the cheese is melted. Remove the scrambled eggs to a plate, and wipe the skillet clean again.

4   To assemble the burritos, lay the tortillas flat on a work surface. Sprinkle the sharp Cheddar cheese evenly down the center of the tortillas, leaving a 2-inch border around the edge. Divide the chorizo, potato mixture, scrambled eggs, and cilantro evenly among the tortillas, spooning over the cheese. Fold opposite sides of the tortilla over the filling, and roll up.

5   Place the skillet over medium-high. Lightly spray each burrito with cooking spray, and cook, seam side down, until lightly browned, 1 to 2 minutes. Turn and cook until lightly browned and the cheese melts, 1 to 2 minutes. Serve immediately with sour cream, pico de gallo, and Sriracha.

Hash Brown Egg Cups

Once upon a time, I wanted to make a Hash Brown Egg Cup but I didn't have potatoes. I sat, shamefully questioning my breakfast-cooking abilities, until I remembered the frozen potato tots I had in my freezer! (Note: I grew up in the Midwest and always have frozen potato tots in my freezer.) It occurred to me that I could thaw those, crisp them up in a skillet with some butter and onions and voilà, a brilliantly yummy Hash Brown Egg Cup was born! The End. Just kidding, I'm not done with this story. These are sweet, these are salty, and an impressive way to make use of frozen ingredients. You should totally make these for your next breakfast gathering. Okay, now I'm done.

1   Preheat the oven to 400°F. Melt the butter in a medium skillet over medium-high. Add the onion, and cook, stirring often, until softened, 5 to 6 minutes. Add the potato tots, and cook, using a wooden spoon to stir and break up the potatoes so they resemble hash browns, about 10 minutes. Remove from the heat.

2   Line a large colander with a few paper towels, and add the hash brown mixture. Wrap up the hash browns with paper towels, and squeeze out as much liquid as you can. Transfer the mixture to a large bowl.

3   Coat 8 cups in a muffin pan with cooking spray. Divide the hash brown mixture evenly among the muffins cups (a few tablespoons each). Using fingers or a rubber spatula, push the potato mixture onto the bottom and up the sides of each cup, creating a tight nest. Spray once more with cooking spray.

4   Bake for 20 minutes. Remove from the oven and crack 1 egg into each cup. Sprinkle evenly with the salt and pepper. Return to the oven, and bake until the whites of the eggs are set and the yolks are to desired degree of doneness, 6 to 8 minutes (you can cook for longer if you prefer a firmer yolk). Sprinkle with avocado and hot sauce for extra flavor hits, if you wish.

SERVES **8**
HANDS-ON TIME: **15 MINUTES**
TOTAL TIME: **40 MINUTES**

¼ cup salted butter

1 small yellow onion, finely diced

4 cups frozen sweet potato tots, thawed

2 cups frozen potato tots, thawed

Cooking spray

8 large eggs

1 teaspoon kosher salt

1 teaspoon black pepper

Diced avocado (optional)

Hot sauce (optional)

SIRIOUSLY **IMPORTANT**

Squeezing the grated potatoes in a paper towel before baking them will remove excess water and make for a crispier hash brown shell.

SIRIOUSLY **VARIED**

You can definitely stick to one potato or the other, depending on your preference. I like to use a combination of sweet potato and regular tots because I feel like it creates a crispier hash brown. You can also experiment by adding veggies or cheese before placing the eggs on top.

Veggie Hash with Crispy Eggs Over Easy

1 small butternut squash, peeled and cut into ½-inch cubes

1 small rutabaga, peeled and cut into ½-inch cubes

1 small fennel bulb, trimmed and cut into ½-inch pieces

6 tablespoons olive oil

1¼ teaspoons kosher salt

¾ teaspoon black pepper

1 bunch Lacinato kale, washed, stemmed, and coarsely chopped

2 garlic cloves, minced

2 teaspoons red wine vinegar

4 large eggs

1 cup baby arugula

2 teaspoons fresh lemon juice

SIRIOUSLY SIMPLE

Use prechopped butternut squash and/or prechopped/bagged kale to save time.

This is one of my favorite things to eat on Breakfast For Dinner nights. Do you have those nights? If so, I think we could be friends. There is nothing better than shaking up a tired weekly routine with a Breakfast Dinner. Brinner. I highly doubt I made that up, but I do think I deserve a round of applause for using it. Brinner isn't just fun for the whole family, it also solves the "Oh no, I have nothing to cook tonight!" dilemma. Do you have eggs? Do you have veggies? You have Brinner. Of course, you can still serve this at breakfast time because it is your life, after all. Whenever you decide to make it, you will fall in love with the earthy, roasted root vegetables, the smoky, sautéed kale, the perfectly cooked eggs and the refreshing, arugula-based salad. Serve it alongside a piece of crusty bread to soak up that runny yolk.

1 Preheat the oven to 400°F. Toss the squash, rutabaga, and fennel with 1½ tablespoons of the olive oil, 1 teaspoon of the kosher salt, and ½ teaspoon of the pepper on a rimmed baking sheet. Spread in a single layer, and bake until the vegetables are lightly caramelized and tender, 30 to 40 minutes.

2 Meanwhile, massage the kale until tender and bright green, about 5 minutes. Heat 1½ tablespoons of the olive oil in a large skillet over medium-high. Add the garlic, and cook 30 seconds. Add the kale, and cook until wilted. Stir in the roasted vegetables and red wine vinegar. Transfer to a bowl, and wipe the skillet clean with a paper towel.

3 Heat 2 tablespoons of the olive oil in the skillet over medium-high. Crack the eggs into the skillet, keeping them separated; sprinkle evenly with the remaining ¼ teaspoon each of salt and pepper. Cook until the edges are crisped and lightly browned, 2 to 3 minutes. Turn the eggs, and immediately remove the skillet from the heat, allowing the eggs to stay in the skillet off the heat until reaching desired degree of doneness.

4 Toss together the arugula, lemon juice, and remaining 1 tablespoon olive oil in a medium bowl until the arugula is well coated. To serve, spoon about 1 cup vegetable hash onto each of 4 plates; top each with 1 egg and about ¼ cup dressed arugula. Serve immediately.

Open-Faced Green Breakfast Sandwich

I cannot figure out what I love most about this sandwich. Is it the crisp, buttery English muffin with a luscious cream cheese and pesto spread? Or is it the delectable egg/avocado/arugula combination? It's probably the cream cheese, because even a small amount gives this sandwich an element of *je ne sais quoi*, which sounds fancy to say. (You know what's not fancy? The fact that I used to eat cream cheese with a spoon in high school.) A drizzle of your favorite hot sauce brightens the dish and gives it a really pretty pop of color. It is extremely simple to make, especially with store-bought pesto, and yet it feels elegant enough to serve at a fancy brunch. You know, those mid-morning gatherings where you invite only your fancy friends over to wear fancy clothes, eat fancy foods and talk about fancy things...like changing diapers?

1 Preheat the broiler to HIGH with the oven rack 6 inches from the heat. Place the English muffin halves, cut sides up, on a baking sheet; spread evenly with 1 tablespoon of the butter. Broil until golden brown, about 2 minutes. Transfer the muffin halves to a plate.

2 Stir together the cream cheese and pesto in a small bowl.

3 Heat a large nonstick skillet over medium-high. Add the remaining 1 tablespoon butter to the skillet; crack the eggs into the skillet, leaving room between the eggs. Cook to desired degree of doneness, about 5 minutes for runny yolks.

4 Spread the cream cheese mixture evenly on the toasted cut sides of the muffin halves; top each with a quarter of the avocado slices. Top each with 1 cooked egg.

5 Toss together the arugula, olive oil, and lemon juice; place about ½ cup of the arugula mixture on each egg. Sprinkle evenly with the salt and pepper, and serve immediately, with Sriracha, if desired.

SERVES **4**
HANDS-ON TIME: **15 MINUTES**
TOTAL TIME: **20 MINUTES**

2 English muffins, split

2 tablespoons unsalted butter, softened

2 ounces cream cheese, softened

1½ tablespoons refrigerated basil pesto

4 large eggs

1 medium-sized ripe avocado, sliced

2 cups packed baby arugula

1 tablespoon extra-virgin olive oil

2 teaspoons fresh lemon juice

¾ teaspoon kosher salt

½ teaspoon black pepper

Sriracha chili sauce (optional)

SIRIOUSLY **FANCY**

Add a few slices of smoked salmon to each breakfast sandwich just on top of the cream cheese layer to heighten the decadence (and fanciness) of this delicious breakfast sandwich stack.

SIRIOUSLY **SIMPLE**

If you have extra cream cheese and pesto, try stirring it into your favorite cooked pasta for an easy weeknight dinner.

SERVES **4**
HANDS-ON TIME: **15 MINUTES**
TOTAL TIME: **20 MINUTES**

2 ripe avocados

**1 tablespoon fresh lemon juice plus
1 teaspoon lemon zest**

¼ teaspoon black pepper

1 ½ teaspoons flaky sea salt

**1 sourdough boule, cut into
4 (¾-inch-thick) slices**

¼ cup extra-virgin olive oil

Cooking spray

4 large eggs

½ teaspoon crushed red pepper

Additional black pepper

SIRIOUSLY MINI

Let the kiddos use their favorite cookie cutters for the egg "holes" to make breakfast more fun. A favorite in our house is Egg-in-Minnesota! (Even though it never ends up looking like the actual state.) Or try making a green face or green hair with the avocado.

Egg-in-Hole Avocado Toast

Can you remember a time when Avocado Toast wasn't a popular breakfast item? I can, even though I prefer not to. In fact, I distinctly remember the first time I experienced the crunchy, yet creamy delight. It was at Swingers Diner in Santa Monica, and it changed my life. How had I not thought of combining avocado with bread before that? Tortilla chips used to be total avocado hogs, if you ask me. Anyway, the trendy toast has now been topped with just about everything, but I prefer to keep mine simple...with a twist, of course. In this recipe, the bright and creamy avocado mixture is combined with a family favorite in our house: egg-in-a-hole. If you're not familiar with that, it's best described as a buttery piece of bread with a hole in the center, toasted to golden perfection on the stove with an egg fried in its center. Egg toast AND avocado?! Take that, tortilla chips.

1 Place the avocados, lemon juice, black pepper, and 1 teaspoon of the salt in a medium bowl. Mash the mixture with a fork, leaving large pieces of the avocado. Set aside.

2 Using a 2-inch biscuit cutter, make a 2-inch hole off center in each sourdough slice. Brush each slice liberally with the olive oil.

3 Heat a large nonstick skillet or griddle over medium. Place the bread slices in the skillet, and cook until golden brown on 1 side, 2 to 3 minutes. Turn the bread, and coat the pan inside the bread holes with cooking spray. Break an egg into each hole. Cover and cook until the whites are set but the yolks are still runny, about 3 minutes. (For over-easy eggs, uncover the skillet, and carefully turn the egg and bread slice. Cook for 20 seconds.) Remove from the skillet.

4 Spread about ½ cup of the avocado mixture next to the egg on each bread slice. Sprinkle evenly with the lemon zest, red pepper, and remaining ½ teaspoon salt. Sprinkle with black pepper and serve immediately.

Spinach, Chickpea, and Tomato Frittata

Some mornings I wake up and crave a hearty brunch. This dish was created on such a morning, but that particular day my fridge appeared empty. I had eggs, and that was about it. Or so I thought...[dramatic pause]. Here's a free tip: When you think you have no food in your house, you have two choices: 1. You can sit and wait for magical elves to appear and stock your house with a bountiful harvest. 2. You can open your freezer and pantry and find treasures you didn't even know were there. I highly recommend you choose number two, because magical elves are expensive and also they aren't real. The point is, this recipe was inspired by pantry and freezer staples like canned chickpeas and frozen spinach. It's a flavorful, filling dish that is great on its own or served on top of crusty bread with a lemony salad.

SERVES **4**
HANDS-ON TIME: **15 MINUTES**
TOTAL TIME: **25 MINUTES**

2 tablespoons olive oil

1 large garlic clove, minced

1 cup halved grape tomatoes

½ (15-ounce) can chickpeas (garbanzo beans), drained and rinsed

1½ teaspoons kosher salt

1 (10-ounce) package frozen chopped spinach, thawed

8 large egg whites

2 tablespoons whole milk

½ teaspoon black pepper

½ teaspoon paprika

1 Preheat the oven to 450°F. Heat the olive oil in an 8-inch ovenproof skillet over medium-high. Add the garlic, and cook, stirring constantly, just until the garlic starts to brown. Add the tomatoes, chickpeas, and ½ teaspoon of the salt, and cook until the tomatoes have slightly wilted, about 5 minutes. Remove from the heat.

2 Using a kitchen towel, squeeze out as much excess liquid from the spinach as you can. Add the spinach to the chickpea mixture in the skillet, and cook over medium-high for 5 minutes, stirring well. Reduce the heat to medium.

3 Place the egg whites in a bowl (save the yolks for another day) and whisk well. Add the milk, pepper, paprika, and remaining 1 teaspoon salt. Whisk until smooth. Pour into the skillet, and cook just until the edges start to set.

4 Transfer the skillet to the oven, and bake, uncovered, until the egg is browned, bubbly, and cooked, 10 to 12 minutes. Transfer the frittata to a plate. Cut into 4 wedges and serve.

SIRIOUSLY SIMPLE

If you'd rather not separate your eggs, you can use 5 whole eggs instead of 8 egg whites. If you do choose the latter method, save those yolks to make yummy pudding with later!

Brown Sugar Peppered Bacon

10 thick-cut bacon slices

⅓ cup packed, plus 2 teaspoons light brown sugar

2 teaspoons black pepper

As a kid, if I ever found myself at a breakfast buffet, I would usually eat close to 10 pieces of bacon. Who let this happen? Where were my parents? Mom, Dad, are you reading this? Even now, it is something I have trouble passing up. We often hang out backstage with Carson at *The Voice*, and if they are ever working early there is typically a delicious breakfast spread complete with, you guessed it, bacon. Sometimes they have a vat of thick, peppered, sugary bacon, and it's close to the best thing I've ever put in my mouth. I knew I could easily recreate this deliciousness at home, and so I did. Guess what? You can, too. It's easy, your entire house will smell divine, and you will impress just about anyone you serve it to. They might even turn their chairs for you! (*Voice* humor.) Only, try hard not to eat 10 pieces at a time.

1 Preheat the oven to 350°F. Line a rimmed baking sheet with aluminum foil. Place a wire rack on the foil. Place as many bacon slices as you can fit on the rack (I usually can get 10 on there).

2 Stir together the brown sugar and pepper in a small bowl. Sprinkle the bacon with the brown sugar mixture, pressing lightly to adhere.

3 Bake until the bacon is CRISPY, 35 to 40 minutes, rotating the baking sheet halfway (on same rack) once or twice during baking time.

I'd always turn my chair for these three :-)

1 cup granulated sugar

½ cup vegetable oil

3 small ripe bananas, mashed

2 teaspoons vanilla extract

½ teaspoon fresh lemon juice

2 large eggs

½ cup whole milk

2 cups all-purpose flour

1 ½ teaspoons baking powder

½ teaspoon kosher salt

Cooking spray

SIRIOUSLY **SINFUL**

Add 1 cup of mini chocolate chips to sweeten them up, as my kids always beg me to do.

Perfect Banana Minimuffins

Photograph on page 36

To claim a recipe is "perfect"—well, it better be that. These muffins are just sweet enough, soft and fluffy and bursting with banana flavor. They are miniature sized, which makes them a convenient breakfast on-the-go or mid-day snack, and you can have them ready to pop in the oven in just ten minutes. See? They are perfection. You will need a mini muffin tin for this recipe, which is one of my favorite kitchen items, but if you'd rather make regular-sized muffins simply increase the baking time by 6 minutes. Look around...I'm sure you have ripe bananas on your counter like I always seem to, and now you know what to do with them!

1   Preheat the oven to 350°F. Whisk together the sugar and oil in a large bowl until smooth. Add the bananas, vanilla, lemon juice, and eggs, and whisk until smooth. Add the milk; whisk until smooth.

2   Stir together the flour, baking powder, and salt. Add the flour mixture to the banana mixture, and stir until just combined. You don't want to over-stir, or you'll have dense muffins.

3   Coat 36 cups in miniature muffin pans with cooking spray. Spoon 1½ tablespoons of the batter into each cup, filling about three-fourths full. Bake until a wooden pick comes out clean, 12 to 14 minutes. Let the muffins cool in the pans for 2 minutes. Remove from the pans to wire racks. Enjoy!

To be clear, that is cookie dough in the bowl, but look at that cute chubber!

Browned Butter Caramelized Banana Bread

Photograph on page 37

Photograph on page 37

MAKES **1 LOAF**
HANDS-ON TIME: **15 MINUTES**
TOTAL TIME: **1 HOUR**
45 MINUTES

The only thing better than baking banana bread is baking caramelized banana bread. Roasting bananas with a little honey and cinnamon transforms the fruit into something incredible—and you don't have to patiently wait for them to turn super ripe prior to baking, because the roasting process will take care of that for you. Also, let's not forget that browning butter takes any recipe over the top. I once spent an entire weekend discussing the magic of browned butter to some friends who had not yet experienced the phenomenon (you know who you are). When you combine the caramelized bananas and the nutty, browned butter, the result is a perfectly moist bread that is simply irresistible. Back to the fact that I spent an entire weekend talking about browning butter...I swear I'm a fun and interesting person.

1 Preheat the oven to 400°F. Place the bananas on a parchment paper-lined baking sheet. Whisk together the honey, oil, and cinnamon until smooth. Drizzle the honey mixture over the bananas, and toss until evenly coated.

2 Bake until the bananas begin to caramelize, about 20 minutes, turning once halfway through. Remove the bananas from the baking sheet, and set aside to cool. Reduce the oven temperature to 350°F.

3 Meanwhile, melt the butter in a small saucepan over medium heat, until the butter begins to brown and have a nutty aroma. Remove from the heat, and set aside to cool.

4 Whisk together the flour, baking powder, salt, baking soda, and nutmeg in a small bowl.

5 Transfer the cooled bananas to a large bowl, and mash. Add the browned butter, brown sugar, sour cream, vanilla, and eggs, and stir until just smooth. Add the dry ingredients, and stir to combine. Pour the batter into a 9 x 5-inch loaf pan greased with butter.

6 Bake until a wooden pick inserted in the center comes out clean, about 1 hour. Cool the bread in the pan for 10 minutes. Remove to a wire rack, and cool completely.

4 ripe bananas, peeled

3 tablespoons honey

1 tablespoon canola oil

³/₄ teaspoon ground cinnamon

6 tablespoons unsalted butter, plus more for greasing pan

1 ¹/₄ cups all-purpose flour

³/₄ teaspoon baking powder

¹/₂ teaspoon kosher salt

¹/₄ teaspoon baking soda

¹/₄ teaspoon ground nutmeg

1 cup packed light brown sugar

¹/₄ cup sour cream

1 teaspoon vanilla extract

2 large eggs, lightly beaten

Perfect Banana
Minimuffins
PG 34

Browned Butter
Caramelized
Banana Bread
PG 35

5-Ingredient Peanut Butter Granola Bars

Do you ever volunteer for too much? Like baking a snack for a bunch of kids on a day that you also have 14 other important things to do? Please tell me your hand is raised and I'm not alone with this quandary. Carson has a saying for me...JUST SAY NO. It's not that he doesn't want me to help out, he just doesn't want me to become an overly stressed, obsessive-compulsive psycho when helping out. This has been known to happen. I sometimes think I can do it all because I'm Super Woman! Mary Poppins! Martha Stewart! However, if you do end up volunteering for that snack job on your busiest day, you can pull off these granola bars with time to spare. They require 5 simple ingredients, 20 minutes of prep time and little to zero effort. The best part is they are rich in protein, low in sugar and taste like a much better version of the store-bought kind. Mary Poppins will be like, "Wait, did you just make homemade granola bars?" "Yes, Poppins," you'll say, "Yes I did."

SERVES **8**

HANDS-ON TIME: **20 MINUTES**

TOTAL TIME: **1 HOUR**

- 1 ½ cups uncooked old-fashioned regular rolled oats
- ⅓ cup crunchy peanut butter
- ⅓ cup honey
- ⅓ cup dates, pitted and finely chopped
- ½ cup crisp rice cereal (such as Rice Krispies)

SIRIOUSLY SINFUL

Stir ½ cup of dark chocolate chips or chopped peanut butter cups into the mixture before baking for an extra-sweet treat.

---

1 Preheat the oven to 350°F. Line an 8-inch square baking pan with parchment paper, allowing the paper to extend over the sides of the pan. Grease the parchment paper.

2 Spread the oats evenly on a rimmed baking sheet, and bake until golden brown, about 15 minutes.

3 Meanwhile, stir together the peanut butter, honey, and dates in a saucepan over medium. Cook, stirring occasionally, until the peanut butter has melted and the dates are well combined, about 5 minutes.

4 Combine the toasted oats and crisp rice cereal in a medium bowl. Pour the peanut butter mixture over the oats and cereal mixture; stir until well blended.

5 Using a rubber spatula, spread the mixture into the prepared pan, pressing lightly into an even layer. Place in the refrigerator, and chill until completely cool and firm, about 30 minutes. Using the parchment paper as handles, lift the chilled bar mixture out of the pan. Cut into 8 rectangles, and serve, or store individually wrapped in plastic wrap for breakfast or snacks.

8 large croissants

2 cups dark chocolate chunks (about 11 ounces)

1 cup roughly chopped toasted pecans

1 ½ cups granulated sugar

8 large eggs

3 cups heavy cream

1 tablespoon vanilla extract

¼ teaspoon kosher salt

2 tablespoons turbinado sugar

SIRIOUSLY **FANCY**

To serve individual bread puddings to dinner guests—because anything mini is "fancy"—divide the bread cubes and torn halves of croissant tops into 12 (10-ounce) ramekins and divide other fillings and sprinkles among ramekins the same way the whole baking dish was assembled. Place the ramekins in a baking pan with water halfway up the sides of the ramekins. Bake at 350°F for 25 to 30 minutes or until set.

Dark Chocolate Croissant Bread Pudding

I am not a donut person. I am a chocolate croissant person. When I was 16, I went to France on a school trip, at which point I contracted a very serious disease called Pain Au Chocolat Syndrome. There is no cure. In fact, the only treatment for such a syndrome is to consume copious amounts of chocolate croissants in one's lifetime. For this reason, I created the following bread pudding for those suffering as I am—or for anyone that loves decadent casseroles starring buttery bread and rich, dark chocolate. Make sure to allow a full hour for the croissants to absorb the cream and eggs, as this will help create a lusciously moist (without being wet) bread pudding. It is the perfect recipe for a Mother's Day brunch (especially if I'm your mother).

1 Slice the croissants in half horizontally, separating the top and bottom halves. Cut the bottom halves into 1-inch cubes, and leave the tops whole.

2 Place the croissant cubes on the bottom of a greased 13 x 9-inch (3-quart) baking dish. Sprinkle with half each of the chocolate chunks and pecans. Place the croissant tops, crust sides up, over the layer of croissant cubes (overlapping slightly, if needed), and top with the remaining chocolate chunks and pecan pieces.

3 Whisk together the granulated sugar and eggs in a large bowl until pale yellow. Whisk in the cream, vanilla, and salt until combined. Pour the mixture over the croissants; cover the dish with plastic wrap and refrigerate for at least 1 hour.

4 Preheat the oven to 350°F. Discard the plastic wrap from the baking dish; place the dish in a roasting pan. Pour hot water into the roasting pan until halfway up the sides of the baking dish. Sprinkle the top of the bread pudding evenly with the turbinado sugar. Bake until golden brown and set in the center, about 1 hour and 15 minutes. Let stand 10 minutes; serve warm.

Spiced Pumpkin Pancakes with Vanilla Whipped Cream

SERVES 6
HANDS-ON TIME: 20 MINUTES
TOTAL TIME: 20 MINUTES

Confession: There is only one food that I cannot stand, and that food is pumpkin pie. Yep, I know, it's like I'm not even an American human being. However, before you throw this book away and curse my name, I like other pumpkin things! In fact, I like ALL the other delicious foods bursting with pumpkin flavor! Friends again? For example, I love these mouthwatering pumpkin pancakes. Each bite is full of warmth and will remind you of a chilly, autumn weekend morning. If you usually make pancakes from a box, you will be surprised how easy they are to make from scratch. Speaking of homemade things, if you've never made your own whipped cream, you must also try that at once (I'm bossy). It is ridiculously easy and so much tastier than the store-bought version. Especially when it's infused with yummy vanilla beans, as it is here. I cannot imagine topping these pancakes with anything else.

½ vanilla bean, split
¾ cup heavy cream
2 tablespoons powdered sugar
1 ½ cups all-purpose flour
2 ¼ teaspoons baking powder
½ teaspoon kosher salt
½ teaspoon ground cinnamon
¼ teaspoon ground nutmeg
1 ¼ cups whole milk
¾ cup canned pumpkin
¼ cup packed light brown sugar
2 tablespoons salted butter, melted
1 teaspoon grated fresh ginger
1 teaspoon orange zest
2 large eggs
Pure maple syrup

1 Scrape the vanilla bean seeds into a bowl; add the cream and powdered sugar. Beat with an electric mixer on medium speed until soft peaks form, about 45 seconds. Refrigerate until ready to serve.

2 Whisk together the flour, baking powder, salt, cinnamon, and nutmeg in a medium bowl. In a separate medium bowl, whisk together the milk, pumpkin, brown sugar, butter, ginger, orange zest, and eggs until smooth; add to the flour mixture. Whisk just until the dry ingredients are moistened.

3 Heat a large nonstick skillet or griddle over medium-high. Scoop the batter by ¼ cupfuls, and drop onto the hot surface; cook until the edges are set and bubbles begin to form on the surface of the batter, 1 to 2 minutes. Turn and cook for 1 minute.

4 To serve, stack 3 pancakes onto each of 6 plates; spoon about ¼ cup of the vanilla whipped cream over each stack. Drizzle with the maple syrup.

SIRIOUSLY MINI

Use a pumpkin cookie cutter to pour the batter into during the cooking process for a fun, autumn-themed breakfast.

TWO

Halftime

Lunch can be a neglected meal. Too often we are eating at our desks, snacking in our cars or skipping it entirely. But then do you know what happens? We become Hangry. This is a word to describe a hungry, angry person. I have been known to be this person, just ask my friends and family. Yes, shocking, I know. You probably assumed I was always happy...a rainbow of unicorns and positive vibes. The truth is, when I'm done with breakfast, I'm already thinking about lunch (and when I'm done with lunch, that's right, I'm already thinking about...lunch number two...just kidding, sort of).

I say all of this because food is very important to me, and if I go too long without it...well, you should watch out. However, there is a way to rid your life of hangry people like me, and that is to eat a proper midday meal.

As much as I wish we all went home around noon, sat down at the table and took our time noshing, followed by a legit European siesta, that is just not the American way. Alas, this does not mean we must eat processed power bars standing up. Quite the opposite! I know a way to B.B.L. ("Bring Back Lunch") or M.L.G.A. ("Make Lunch Great Again")*. It's a straightforward solution: If you are able to spend an hour or two on the weekend prepping some Chicken Parmigiana Burgers, making a hefty pot of Crab-and-Corn Chowder or a big bowl of Italian Orecchiette Pasta Salad, you can easily whip together lunches as your week unfolds.

Of course, I am aware that it is not always that simple. Sometimes weekends end up busier than your week, or on the flip side, they are so lazy that you don't want to lift a finger! That's why in this chapter there is a lunch that fits any scenario. For the kiddos, you can quickly throw together the Apple, Nut Butter, and Granola Sandwiches or the Bacon Pizzadillas, and for yourself nothing is easier or more sinfully delicious than a Caramelized Brussels Sprouts Grilled Cheese. If you have a little more time to spend, the Buddha Bowls will elevate any lunch shindig, and for a football Sunday, Lucy's Sticky Ham Sandwiches will be an instant hit. Within these pages, there is a salad, sandwich, soup and burger for anyone.

So the next time you find yourself thinking, Should I eat fast food today? Should I try and power through until dinnertime? Should I force my kids to buy hot lunch? (Which, by the way, I totally approve and repeatedly take advantage of.) Instead of answering yes to these questions, pick up this book and page through these recipes and Make Lunch Great Again.

*Can someone please make these abbreviations "a thing?" Thanks.

2 medium-sized red beets

2 medium-sized golden beets

2 tablespoons white wine vinegar

1 tablespoon Dijon mustard

½ teaspoon kosher salt

¼ teaspoon black pepper

¼ cup extra-virgin olive oil

10 ounces arugula

1 ripe avocado, sliced

¼ cup toasted pine nuts

¼ cup shaved Parmesan cheese

Roasted Beet-and-Arugula Salad

I am guilty of breezing by lunch on busy days, and honestly, aren't all days busy days? The problem is that if I skip a meal, I turn into my alter ego—Hangry Mom. NO ONE likes Hangry Mom. She is short-tempered, impatient and might even eat a pebble off the street, that's how hangry she is. Luckily, there is a way to avoid her evil presence, and that is to prep simple ingredients for quick lunch assembly. Roasting beets on a Sunday is one of my favorite things to do because I know that during the week I can whip up this salad on a moment's notice. The earthy flavor of beets is so perfect with smooth, creamy avocado, and the Dijon mustard vinaigrette balances out the dish with just enough acidity. Topped with crunchy pine nuts and salty Parmesan cheese...Hangry Mom will be gone forever (or, like, until after dinner when she really needs dessert).

1   Preheat the oven to 425°F. Leave the root and 1 inch of stem on the beets; scrub with a brush. Fill a baking dish ¼ inch deep with water, and add the beets. Cover tightly with aluminum foil, and bake until tender, about 1 hour and 10 minutes. Cool for about 20 minutes. Peel, and cut into wedges.

2   Whisk together the vinegar, Dijon, salt, and pepper in a small bowl until combined. Slowly drizzle in the olive oil, whisking constantly until combined. Arrange the beet slices in a single layer on a platter; drizzle with half of the vinegar mixture.

3   Combine the arugula and avocado in a large bowl. Drizzle with the remaining vinegar mixture, and toss gently to coat. Top the beets with the arugula salad and sprinkle with the pine nuts and cheese.

Italian Orecchiette Pasta Salad

SERVES 6

HANDS-ON TIME: **20 MINUTES**

TOTAL TIME: **30 MINUTES**

Pasta salad was the first thing I learned to cook in my Home Economics class when I was in 7th grade. I immediately came home and made it for my younger siblings. They were picky eaters, and because there were some vegetables in it, they wouldn't touch it. I'm pretty sure I threw a tantrum and swore I would never talk to them again. I'm also pretty sure they didn't care about that threat. Regardless, I still have a fondness for pasta salad, perhaps because it is such a foolproof way to throw a delicious lunch together. This recipe is rich in flavor, color and texture. It's easy to make in bulk for a luncheon or to stock your fridge for quick midday meals. Whether you eat it warm so that the cheese melts slightly, or cold over a bed of spring greens, you will love this lunch. (If not, I'll never talk to you again.)

1 Cook the pasta according to the package directions for al dente; drain. Place the pasta in a large bowl, and let cool for 10 minutes.

2 Meanwhile, whisk together the oil, vinegar, lemon juice, salt, and pepper in a small bowl.

3 Add the salami, cucumber, tomatoes, mozzarella, olives, onion, and parsley to the pasta. Drizzle with the dressing, and toss gently to coat. Sprinkle with the grated Parmigiano-Reggiano, and serve.

8 ounces uncooked orecchiette pasta

½ cup extra-virgin olive oil

3 tablespoons white wine vinegar

1 ½ tablespoons fresh lemon juice (from 1 lemon)

¾ teaspoon kosher salt

¼ teaspoon black pepper

1 (6-ounce) salami, cubed

½ English cucumber, seeded and cubed

1 pint heirloom or multicolored cherry tomatoes, halved

4 ounces fresh mozzarella cheese, cut into ½-inch cubes (about 1 cup)

½ cup pitted kalamata olives, halved

½ cup chopped red onion

¼ cup chopped fresh flat-leaf parsley

¼ cup grated Parmigiano-Reggiano cheese

2 cups diced peeled sweet potato (from 2 medium potatoes)

1 bunch Broccolini, stems removed

¼ cup extra-virgin olive oil

1 ¾ teaspoons kosher salt, plus more for seasoning

½ teaspoon black pepper, plus more for seasoning

1 bunch Lacinato kale, stems removed, leaves chopped

1 (15-ounce) can chickpeas (garbanzo beans), drained, rinsed, and outer skins removed

½ teaspoon ground cumin

½ teaspoon chili powder

1 garlic clove, minced

1 tablespoon vegetable oil

2 cups cooked wild rice or brown rice

1 medium-sized ripe avocado, halved and sliced

2 teaspoons olive oil

Hot sauce (optional)

Buddha Bowls

Buddha Bowls, also known as Hippie Bowls, are hearty vessels made up of raw and roasted veggies, usually dark, leafy greens, and beans or rice. I think the idea is they are full of nutritious ingredients that make your belly happy and full. In this recipe, sweet potato, Broccolini and kale are roasted together for a textural and flavorful base, and then added to your favorite cooked rice. Avocado lends the perfect creaminess, and the seasoned and sautéed garbanzo beans balance out the bowl with a slight crunch. This is veggie comfort food at its finest. It will make you want to hug a tree or rub your plump belly with glee.

1 Preheat the oven to 400°F. Place the sweet potatoes and Broccolini on a large rimmed baking sheet. Drizzle with the extra-virgin olive oil, and sprinkle with 1 ½ teaspoons of the salt and ½ teaspoon black pepper. Roast for 15 minutes. Stir in the kale, and roast until lightly browned and the kale is wilted, about 5 minutes. Remove and cover with aluminum foil; set aside.

2 Meanwhile, toss together the chickpeas, cumin, chili powder, garlic, and ¼ teaspoon of the salt in a large bowl.

3 Heat the vegetable oil in a skillet over medium. Add the chickpea mixture, and cook, stirring often, until the chickpeas have a nice crunch, 10 to 15 minutes.

4 Divide the rice between 2 bowls. Top evenly with the roasted veggies, chickpea mixture, and avocado. Drizzle each serving with about 1 teaspoon olive oil, and, if desired, hot sauce. Season with salt and pepper, and serve immediately.

SIRIOUSLY **SIMPLE**

I often double or triple the batch of crispy garbanzo beans because I love them for snacking purposes or tossed with weekday salads.

Perfect Chopped Salad

SERVES **8**
HANDS-ON TIME: **20 MINUTES**
TOTAL TIME: **20 MINUTES**

I love a good chopped salad. It's a convenient way to use your fresh produce, and it makes a delicious lunch. However, I have some rules. Oh yes, I always have rules. When I was a kid I wanted to write a handbook called *The Proper Etiquette of Christmas Lights*. Yep, I named it that. Okay, salad rules: If you follow these 5 simple steps like the recipe below does, you will always end up with a perfect chopped salad.

SIZE: Nothing bothers me more than a salad with giant pieces of lettuce or long, chunky vegetables that need to be cut with a knife. If everything is proportional, a perfect bite with everything the salad has to offer is much more attainable.

HERBS: Basil, cilantro, parsley, mint, etc: These herbs can turn a good salad into a great salad by making everything taste fresh and vibrant.

CRUNCH: Certain lettuces and vegetables offer a nice crunch, but I need more than that. I need nuts or seeds or croutons or crushed tortilla chips. My go-to is toasted pine nuts for the subtly sweet, nutty flavor and of course, the crunch.

CITRUS: Much like herbs, citrus adds a vibrancy and freshness to the salad and brings out all the flavors of the vegetables.

DRESSING: Making your own dressing is much less intimidating than it may seem. Oils, vinegars, citrus, mustards, herbs, garlic, etc.—mixing and matching a combination of these ingredients will result in an impressive and tasty homemade dressing.

1   Make the Dressing: Whisk together the vinegar, lemon juice, Dijon, salt, and pepper in a medium bowl until well blended. Slowly drizzle in the olive oil, whisking constantly until combined. Set aside.

2   Make the Salad: Prepare the haricots verts according to the package directions, and then cut into 1-inch pieces. Combine all of the Salad ingredients in a large bowl. Drizzle the Dressing over the Salad, and toss to coat. Serve immediately.

DRESSING

3 tablespoons white balsamic vinegar

1 tablespoon fresh lemon juice

2 teaspoons Dijon mustard

½ teaspoon kosher salt

¼ teaspoon black pepper

½ cup olive oil

SALAD

1 (8-ounce) package steam-in-bag haricots verts

1 (16-ounce) can chickpeas (garbanzo beans), drained and rinsed

5 small radishes, quartered

2 romaine lettuce hearts, chopped

1 English cucumber, cut into ½-inch pieces

½ head radicchio, chopped

¾ cup fresh corn kernels

¼ cup loosely packed fresh basil leaves, torn

¼ cup loosely packed fresh mint leaves, torn

⅓ cup frozen green peas, thawed

⅓ cup toasted sliced almonds

1 pound ground turkey

¼ cup panko (Japanese-style breadcrumbs)

2 tablespoons finely chopped yellow onion

1 teaspoon kosher salt

½ teaspoon black pepper

1 large egg, lightly beaten

2 garlic cloves, minced

½ cup chopped fresh flat-leaf parsley

3 tablespoons olive oil

3 carrots, thinly sliced

1 medium-sized sweet onion, chopped

2 garlic cloves, minced

2 (32-ounce) containers chicken broth

3 cups chopped escarole

¼ cup grated Parmesan cheese

SIRIOUSLY MINI

Make a double batch of meatballs to serve over pasta for the kids. Simply skip the browning step and bake them on a baking sheet in a 400°F oven for 20 minutes.

Italian Wedding Soup

If I were 10, I would tell you that I love this soup so much, I might marry it. Good thing I am a grown-up woman and have no room for silly puns like that in my life (says the woman who named her blog and book SIRIously Delicious). Instead, I will tell you why I adore this pot of warmth and flavor. It begins with the turkey meatballs, which are delightful on their own. While all-white turkey meat is leanest, I usually buy ground dark meat for more depth of flavor. The tender meatballs are browned first, and then simmered in a broth with carrots, onions, garlic and leafy escarole. Finish it off with freshly grated Parmesan, serve it alongside some crusty bread, and you are left with a lunch they write love songs about.

1   Combine the ground turkey, panko, onion, salt, pepper, egg, garlic, and 2 tablespoons of the parsley in a medium bowl. Shape into 30 (1-inch) meatballs (about 1 level tablespoonful each).

2   Heat 1 tablespoon of the oil in a Dutch oven over medium. Add half of the meatballs, and cook, turning occasionally, until browned on all sides, 3 to 4 minutes. Transfer the meatballs to a plate. Repeat with 1 tablespoon of the oil and remaining meatballs.

3   Add the remaining 1 tablespoon oil to the Dutch oven, and heat over medium-high. Add the carrots, onion, and garlic, and cook, stirring occasionally, until almost tender, about 15 minutes. Stir in the broth, and bring to a boil, stirring occasionally. Reduce the heat to medium, stir in the escarole, and simmer, stirring occasionally, until almost tender, 5 to 7 minutes. Stir in the meatballs and simmer, stirring occasionally, until the meatballs are thoroughly cooked, 5 to 7 minutes. Stir in the remaining 6 tablespoons parsley, and sprinkle each serving with cheese.

6 bacon slices

2 celery stalks, diced

1 medium-sized yellow onion, diced

1 large carrot, diced

2 cups fresh corn kernels

1 medium russet potato, peeled and cubed

1/2 teaspoon kosher salt

1/4 teaspoon black pepper

1/4 teaspoon paprika

1 (32-ounce) container chicken broth

3 tablespoons all-purpose flour

1 pound fresh lump crabmeat, drained and picked over

1 cup heavy cream

1/4 cup chopped fresh cilantro, plus more for garnish

SIRIOUSLY SIMPLE

Use frozen or canned corn kernels rather than fresh.

SIRIOUSLY SINFUL

Use lobster instead of crab for a fancy dinner party.

Crab-and-Corn Chowder

Photograph on page 60

Does food ever trigger a memory for you? It should, and if it doesn't, you're doing it wrong (#bossy). Chowders always remind me of the time I spent as a child on the East Coast. We lived in Connecticut not far from the water, and chowders were so popular, especially during the colder months. I distinctly remember trying my first seafood chowder and proudly proclaiming that I loved fish! Of course, that meant I would eat seafood chowders and tuna casserole, period. Still, I'm sure my mother was happy that my palate would accept a soup like this one, starring sweet lumps of crab, crisp corn kernels and tender potatoes. The cilantro adds freshness, and the bacon completes the dish with a salty crunch. It is creamy, it is luscious, and it should be enjoyed anywhere, anytime (#stillbossy).

1   Cook the bacon in a Dutch oven over medium until crisp, 8 to 10 minutes. Transfer to a plate lined with paper towels; reserve 2 tablespoons of the drippings in the Dutch oven.

2   Add the celery, onion, and carrot to the drippings, and cook, over medium, stirring often, until softened, about 8 minutes. Stir in the corn, potato, salt, pepper, and paprika, and cook for 2 minutes.

3   Whisk together the broth and flour in a bowl until smooth; stir into the vegetable mixture. Bring to a boil, reduce the heat to medium-low, and simmer, stirring occasionally, until the vegetables are tender and the mixture has thickened, about 15 minutes. Gently stir in the crabmeat, cream, and cilantro and cook until heated through, about 2 minutes. Crumble the bacon, and sprinkle over each serving, with more cilantro, if desired.

Leftover Veggie Soup with Homemade Croutons

Photograph on page 61

Photograph on page 61

Does the thought of making soup intimidate you? Don't let it! Come here, hold my hand, we will get through this together. While it might seem daunting, throwing together a big batch of steamy soup is actually one of the easiest culinary accomplishments. You almost can't go wrong, as long as you develop the flavors first by sautéing your base with seasonings before adding your broth. I call this "Leftover Veggie Soup" because you can utilize any vegetable you have in your fridge. By decreasing the cooking time, you will not only avoid mushy soup, you will also have lunch ready in no time. The homemade croutons offer the perfect crunch to this light and refreshing meal. See? No more soup scaries. (That's a thing.)

1 Make the Croutons: Preheat the oven to 350°F. Whisk together the butter, oil, salt, pepper, and garlic powder in a large bowl. Add the baguette cubes, and toss to coat. Spread evenly on a rimmed baking sheet. Bake until golden brown, about 15 minutes.

2 Make the Soup: Heat the oil in a Dutch oven over medium-high. Add the carrots, celery, and onion and cook until the vegetables are softened, about 10 minutes. Add the garlic, thyme, salt, and pepper, and cook, stirring constantly, for 1 minute. Stir in the broth, broccoli, corn, tomatoes, and zucchini, and bring to a boil. Remove from the heat. Serve immediately topped with the Croutons.

SERVES **8**
HANDS-ON TIME: **35 MINUTES**
TOTAL TIME: **35 MINUTES**

CROUTONS

2 tablespoons salted butter, melted

2 tablespoons extra-virgin olive oil

½ teaspoon kosher salt

¼ teaspoon black pepper

¼ teaspoon garlic powder

3 cups diced baguette

SOUP

1 tablespoon olive oil

2 medium carrots, chopped

2 celery stalks, chopped

1 large sweet onion, chopped

3 garlic cloves, minced

2 teaspoons chopped fresh thyme

1¼ teaspoons kosher salt

½ teaspoon black pepper

2 (32-ounce) containers chicken or vegetable broth

1 (8-ounce) bag fresh broccoli florets

1 cup fresh corn kernels

2 plum tomatoes, seeded and chopped

1 medium zucchini, quartered lengthwise and sliced

SIRIOUSLY **SIMPLE**

Use frozen corn, a can of diced tomatoes, or dried herbs instead of fresh.

SIRIOUSLY **MINI**

Add some alphabet pasta that kids always love!

Crab-and-Corn
Chowder
PG 58

Leftover Veggie Soup with
Homemade Croutons
PG 59

Creamy Chicken Tortilla Soup

SERVES **6**

HANDS-ON TIME: **30 MINUTES**

TOTAL TIME: **45 MINUTES**

This is one of my all-time favorite soups. The recipe is straightforward, the ingredients are easy to find and it makes a hearty, delicious lunch. It is full of great Mexican flavors and smooth, creamy textures. It reminds me of my good friend who orders this type of soup at any Mexican restaurant. You can utilize leftover or store-bought chicken, canned tomatoes and frozen corn. Shortcuts like that are always key. I could go on and on listing the reasons I love this soup, but instead I encourage you to make it and come up with your own reasons. Then call me (just kidding, I hate the phone; send me an email), because I'd like to hear them all.

1   Heat the olive oil in a large saucepan over medium. Add the carrots, celery, onion, and garlic and cook, stirring often, until softened, about 5 minutes.

2   Add the cilantro, cumin, paprika, chili powder, salt, and pepper, and cook, stirring constantly, for 30 seconds. Add the flour, and cook, stirring often, until the flour is golden, about 1 minute. Stir in the tomatoes, and bring to a simmer.

3   Stir in the cream until combined. Stir in the chicken stock, and bring to a boil.

4   Remove from the heat and, using a handheld immersion blender, process until smooth or desired consistency is reached. (I like mine still somewhat chunky.)

5   Return to medium, and stir in the chicken and corn. Simmer until the chicken is heated through and the corn is tender, about 15 minutes. Serve with toppings of your choice!

2 tablespoons olive oil

½ cup diced carrot

⅓ cup diced celery

1 cup diced yellow onion

1 garlic clove, minced

1 tablespoon chopped fresh cilantro

1 teaspoon ground cumin

1 teaspoon paprika

1 teaspoon chili powder

1 teaspoon kosher salt

½ teaspoon black pepper

2 teaspoons all-purpose flour

1 (28-ounce) can crushed tomatoes, drained

2 tablespoons half-and-half, heavy cream, or milk

4 cups chicken stock

3 cups shredded rotisserie chicken

1 cup frozen corn kernels

Toppings: sour cream, tortilla chips, queso fresco, chopped fresh cilantro

SIRIOUSLY NUTRITIOUS

You can omit the cream if you don't want a creamy soup.

SIRIOUSLY SIMPLE

If you don't have a handheld immersion blender, transfer the soup to a blender to puree, working in batches.

SIRIOUSLY FANCY

Make your own tortilla chips for topping this soup. Simply chop flour or corn tortillas into strips, toss with a few tablespoons of oil, season with salt, pepper and paprika, and toast on a baking sheet in a 350°F oven for 10 minutes or so, until golden and crispy.

Apple, Nut Butter, and Granola Sandwiches

⅓ cup creamy almond butter or other nut butter

1 large Granny Smith apple, cored and sliced crosswise into 8 rings

¼ cup granola

2 tablespoons golden raisins

We have spent a lot of time at NBC's *The Voice* over the years. When the show premiered, our son Jackson was only two years old, which is mind-boggling for me. It's common for coaches, staff and crew to bring their kids to work, so the backstage area sometimes feels like a daycare. Getting kids to eat nutritious foods when they are tempted by treats and junk food isn't easy, which is why I'm always grateful to find these apple sandwiches at the snack table on set. They are packed with energy and protein, and they are finger-food at its finest. Along with being sweet, salty, crunchy and tart, they are an ideal lunch for quick, busy kids (or adults) who only want to have fun.

Spread about ¾ tablespoon of almond butter onto 4 of the apple rings. Sprinkle each with 1 tablespoon granola and about ½ tablespoon raisins. Top with the remaining 4 apple rings; press gently to form sandwiches.

SIRIOUSLY MINI

Kids don't like raisins? Replace with mini chocolate chips—at least they're still eating fruit!

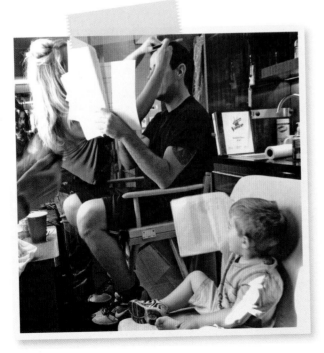

Real men wear makeup, son.

Grilled Cheese Roll-Up Dippers

East Coast winters have been known to produce many a blizzard. Last year, on one particular snow day, I grabbed my skis (nope) and trekked over to my neighbor Jen's house to keep her company. Her teenage daughter had an army of friends over to celebrate no school, so I sat in her kitchen while she cranked out snack after snack, hot tomato soup and these Grilled Cheese Roll-Up Dippers. The recipe is simple, but they're such a fun twist on traditional melted cheese sandwiches. Here, they are served with an easy, flavor-rich marinara dipping sauce. They make the perfect kid-friendly lunch or snack and with simple, minimal ingredients, you can churn out a bunch the next winter day you are stuck indoors with a million children.

1   Make the Marinara: Heat the oil in a saucepan over medium. Add the garlic, and cook, stirring constantly, for 1 minute. Add the tomato paste and cook, stirring constantly, for another minute. Stir in the crushed tomatoes, reduce the heat to low, and simmer for 10 minutes. Remove from the heat. Stir in the chopped fresh basil, salt, and pepper; cover to keep warm.

2   Make the Roll-Up Dippers: Heat a griddle or nonstick skillet over medium. Flatten the bread slices with a rolling pin. Spread 1 1/2 teaspoons of butter on 1 side of each bread slice. Place the bread slices, buttered sides down, on wax or parchment paper. Top each with 1 cheese slice, and roll up the bread; place on the wax paper, seam sides down.

3   Place the Roll-Ups on the preheated griddle, seam sides down, in batches. Cook, turning with a spatula to brown all sides, until the cheese is melted, about 4 minutes. Serve immediately with the Marinara dipping sauce.

SERVES **6**
HANDS-ON TIME: **25 MINUTES**
TOTAL TIME: **25 MINUTES**

MARINARA

2 tablespoons olive oil

2 garlic cloves, minced

1 1/2 tablespoons tomato paste

1 (14 1/2-ounce) can crushed tomatoes

2 tablespoons chopped fresh basil

1/2 teaspoon kosher salt

1/2 teaspoon black pepper

ROLL-UP DIPPERS

12 soft whole-wheat bread slices, crusts removed

6 tablespoons salted butter, softened

12 American, Muenster, or Cheddar cheese slices

SIRIOUSLY SINFUL

For adult grilled cheese dippers, use multiple cheeses such as pepper Jack, sharp Cheddar, and mozzarella paired with any or all of the following: pesto, caramelized onions, roasted red peppers sautéed mushrooms—the list can go on and on.

Caramelized Brussels Sprouts Grilled Cheese

2 tablespoons unsalted butter, softened

¼ cup shredded Brussels sprouts

2 tablespoons chopped yellow onion

¼ teaspoon kosher salt

⅛ teaspoon black pepper

2 bread slices

2 white Cheddar cheese slices

I went to college in Wisconsin, so cheese is sort of my thing. Sure, some may grow up apprenticing at fromageries in France, claiming cheese is their thing, but spending four years going to football games with Cheese Heads while snacking on cheese curds truly makes you an expert. So let's talk about cheese, shall we? This is not your ordinary grilled cheese sandwich. This recipe was born on a football Sunday—let's pretend we were watching the Green Bay Packers (even though it was definitely the Oakland Raiders)—and we were hungry. I had some leftover shredded Brussels sprouts so I decided to sauté them with butter and onions, a heavenly thing to do. Then, my inner cheese expertise guided me to place the veggies between two pieces of buttery bread with sharp, white Cheddar cheese. Best. Decision. Ever. This gooey, cheesy sandwich tastes like a sinful lunch but hey, you're still getting some veggies. On Wisconsin!

1 Heat 1 tablespoon of the butter in a small skillet over medium. Add the Brussels sprouts and onion, and sprinkle with salt and pepper. Cook, stirring often, until brown and caramelized, 6 to 7 minutes. Transfer the Brussels sprouts mixture to a bowl.

2 Spread ½ tablespoon of the remaining butter on 1 side of each bread slice. Place the bread, buttered sides down, in the skillet.

3 Place 1 cheese slice on the bread, and top with the Brussels sprouts mixture. Add the remaining cheese slice, and top with the remaining bread slice, buttered side up.

4 Cook over medium heat until golden brown and the cheese is melted, about 2 minutes per side.

Chickpea Burgers

We are big fans of chickpeas at our house, or you might call them garbanzo beans (but "chickpea" is more fun to say and write). I throw them on almost any salad as an added source of protein, but this recipe was born from a desire to do more with them. They deserve more! Introducing...Chickpea Burgers: a hearty, vegetarian lunch featuring well-seasoned chickpeas, mushrooms and carrots. They are formed into patties, cooked until crisp and served on soft buns with optional toppings like feta cheese, sliced cucumber or creamy tzatziki sauce. This solid meal will forever change the way you look at a can of chickpeas, as they have so much to offer your lunchtime routine.

1 Pulse the chickpeas, garlic, cilantro, cumin, coriander, salt, and pepper in a food processor or blender until the mixture reaches a choppy, paste-like consistency, 5 to 6 times. Using a rubber spatula, transfer the mixture to a large bowl.

2 Pulse the mushrooms and carrots in the food processor until finely minced, 7 to 8 times; add to the chickpea mixture. Stir in the panko, flour, and egg until combined. Divide the mixture into 4 equal portions, and shape each portion into a 1-inch-thick patty.

3 Heat the oil in a large skillet over medium-high. Add the patties, and cook until nice and golden brown, about 6 minutes per side. Serve on hamburger buns with your desired toppings.

SERVES 4
HANDS-ON TIME: 20 MINUTES
TOTAL TIME: 35 MINUTES

1 (16-ounce) can chickpeas (garbanzo beans), drained and rinsed

1 garlic clove

2 tablespoons chopped fresh cilantro or flat-leaf parsley

1 ½ teaspoons ground cumin

1 ½ teaspoons ground coriander

1 teaspoon kosher salt

½ teaspoon black pepper

8 ounces fresh cremini mushrooms, sliced

2 medium carrots, chopped

¼ cup panko (Japanese-style breadcrumbs)

2 tablespoons all-purpose flour

1 large egg

2 tablespoons olive oil

4 hamburger buns

Toppings: feta cheese, sliced tomato, sliced red onion, lettuce, sliced cucumbers, tzatziki sauce

3 tablespoons olive oil

8 ounces fresh cremini mushrooms, finely chopped

1 cup diced yellow onion

1 garlic clove, minced

1 teaspoon Worcestershire sauce

1 cup cooked lentils

1 cup fresh breadcrumbs

1 large egg, lightly beaten

1 teaspoon kosher salt

½ teaspoon black pepper

4 hamburger buns

Toppings: lettuce, sliced red onion, mayonnaise, Dijon mustard

SIRIOUSLY IMPORTANT

It's important to purée half of the lentils, which will bind the burgers together nicely, resulting in a crusty exterior.

Mushroom and Lentil Burgers

I am self-admittedly a meat lover; however, a good veggie burger is hard to pass up. This particular recipe, featuring mushrooms and lentils, is meaty in texture and flavor, and will win the hearts of carnivores and plant-eaters alike! It's all about balance, after all, which is what I'm going to boldly tattoo on my forehead one day. This dish is heavy in protein and light in fat, full in flavor and lacking in calories. Balance. I would serve it alongside some sweet potato fries because, as my forehead clearly states, balance is key.

1   Heat 1 tablespoon of the olive oil in a large skillet over medium. Add the mushrooms, onion, and garlic, and cook, stirring constantly, until the mushrooms are browned, the garlic is lightly toasted, and the onion is translucent, about 7 minutes.

2   Stir in the Worcestershire sauce, and remove from the heat. Cool for 5 minutes.

3   Process ½ cup of the lentils in a food processor until smooth, about 30 seconds. Stir together the mushroom mixture, breadcrumbs, egg, salt, pepper, pureed lentils, and remaining whole lentils in a large bowl.

4   Divide the mixture into 4 equal portions and shape each into a 1-inch-thick patty. Place the patties on a platter, cover with plastic wrap, and chill for 30 minutes.

5   Heat the remaining 2 tablespoons olive oil in a large skillet over medium-high. Add the patties, and cook until crispy, 5 to 7 minutes per side. Serve on hamburger buns with your desired toppings.

Chicken Parmigiana Burgers

SERVES **4**
HANDS-ON TIME: **20 MINUTES**
TOTAL TIME: **35 MINUTES**

Guess what, you guys? I live in Chicken Parm Country. It's true. I've even seen people fly flags with images of Chicken Parmesan on them. That is not true. However, the truth is that you can find the irresistible dish at countless delis and restaurants in my 'hood. While it's very tasty, I'm not always in the mood for the fried chicken loaded with heavy sauce and cheese. These Chicken Parmigiana Burgers are a lighter, healthier alternative with just as much flavor. You take lean ground chicken, combine it with Greek yogurt, panko breadcrumbs, Parmesan cheese and lots of spices, brown them on the stove, and then pop them in the broiler with tomatoes, sauce, and cheese. They make a delicious and filling lunch, with or without the bun. Fly that Chicken Parm Burger Flag high, my friends!

1 pound ground chicken

½ cup panko (Japanese-style breadcrumbs)

½ cup nonfat Greek yogurt

⅓ cup grated Parmesan cheese

1 teaspoon chopped fresh thyme

1 teaspoon chopped fresh rosemary

1 teaspoon chopped fresh basil, plus leaves for garnish

1 teaspoon kosher salt

½ teaspoon chopped fresh oregano

½ teaspoon black pepper

6 garlic cloves, minced

¼ teaspoon crushed red pepper (optional)

2 tablespoons olive oil

1 cup tomato sauce

1 large tomato, cut into 4 slices

4 buffalo mozzarella cheese slices

4 hamburger buns

1   Place the chicken, panko, yogurt, Parmesan, thyme, rosemary, basil, salt, oregano, black pepper, garlic, and, if desired, crushed red pepper in a bowl, and gently combine, using a spoon or your hands.

2   Divide the chicken mixture into 4 equal portions; shape each into a 1-inch-thick patty. Heat the olive oil in a large skillet over medium-high. Add the patties, and cook until a golden brown crust forms, about 6 minutes per side.

3   Preheat the broiler. Place the patties on a baking sheet. Spoon about ¼ cup of the tomato sauce onto each burger. Top each with 1 tomato slice and 1 cheese slice.

4   Broil for a couple of minutes, until the cheese is melted and bubbly. Serve on hamburger buns with extra basil, if desired.

SIRIOUSLY **SIMPLE**

If you can't find ground chicken, ask someone in the grocery store's meat department or at your butcher shop to grind a mix of boneless breast and thigh.

½ cup unsalted butter

1 tablespoon dry mustard

1 tablespoon Worcestershire sauce

2 tablespoons light brown sugar

1 tablespoon poppy seeds

1 (12-ounce) package small sweet Hawaiian rolls

1 pound sliced deli ham

1 pound Swiss cheese, sliced

SIRIOUSLY **SIMPLE**

I like to use disposable baking dishes for easy clean up, and for the fact that I am almost always transporting these sandwiches to some sort of football tailgate. Sweet Hawaiian rolls are easy to slice all at once as long as you use a long serrated knife and you don't pull them apart before cutting.

SIRIOUSLY **VARIED**

If you're not a fan of Swiss cheese, really any alternative would work well. You can also experiment with sliced turkey or roast beef.

Lucy's Sticky Ham Sandwiches

Before we can talk about how good these sandwiches are, you must first get to know the woman behind them. Lucy was my friend's mother and my mother's friend. She lit up every room with her kind spirit and giant smile. She raised four beautiful children, cared for her many grandchildren, worked as a teacher, kicked butt on the tennis court and cooked incredible food. As it does to so many, Alzheimer's tragically took her life way too soon, but her memory lives on in all who knew her. These sticky ham sandwiches of hers were a staple at any gathering growing up, and I'm so glad that over the years my blog has spread them into the homes of people who never knew Lucy. She would have loved knowing that her addictive recipe has become a go-to in so many kitchens. Anyone who tries these sweet and savory sandwiches will beg you for the recipe. Just be certain to make enough, because there won't be any leftovers!

1 Bring the butter, dry mustard, Worcestershire sauce, brown sugar, and poppy seeds to a boil in a medium saucepan over medium-high. Reduce the heat to medium-low, and simmer for 5 minutes. Set aside.

2 Split the rolls. Layer the ham and cheese slices evenly on the bottom halves of the rolls, then cover with the top halves of the rolls. Place the rolls in a single layer in an 11- x 7-inch baking dish. (It helps if they fit snugly in there.) Pour the sauce over the buns, using a spatula to make sure they are all coated. Cover with aluminum foil, and chill for at least 1 hour or up to overnight.

3 Preheat the oven to 325°F. Bake the sandwiches, covered, for 10 minutes. Uncover and bake until the sandwiches are hot and the cheese is melted, about 10 more minutes.

Bacon Pizzadillas

My husband is an idea man. He deserves credit for inspiring so many of my recipes, because his brain is always simmering up new and interesting ways to improve basic food. While "pizzadillas" may not be revolutionary, when Carson suggested I try them, our entire family gave him a jolly old pat on the back. My daughter Etta asks for quesadillas almost daily, so any variation on the classic version is welcome in my kitchen. This recipe features mozzarella cheese, pizza sauce and crispy bacon. When your son owns bacon t-shirts and pizza shorts, you know these will be an instant hit. Hmm, it's really mind-boggling where Carson gets all these great ideas from...

1 Cook the bacon in a large nonstick skillet over medium, stirring occasionally, until crisp, 5 to 6 minutes. Transfer to a plate lined with paper towels. Wipe the skillet clean.

2 Heat the butter in the skillet over medium; swirl to coat.

3 Top each tortilla with about 4½ tablespoons pizza sauce, spreading evenly with a spatula. Sprinkle the tortillas evenly with the mozzarella, crumbled bacon, oregano, and garlic powder. If desired, add a pinch of crushed red pepper to each tortilla.

4 Place 1 tortilla in the skillet, topping side up. Cook until the cheese starts to melt and the tortilla starts to puff, 30 seconds to 1 minute.

5 Using a spatula, fold the tortilla in half, and continue to cook, flipping occasionally, until both sides are brown, 1 to 2 minutes. Remove and slice into 4 pieces. Repeat with the remaining tortillas.

SERVES **6**
HANDS-ON TIME: **15 MINUTES**
TOTAL TIME: **20 MINUTES**

6 bacon slices, diced

1 teaspoon unsalted butter

6 (8-inch) flour tortillas

1 (14-ounce) jar pizza sauce

8 ounces mozzarella cheese, shredded

2 teaspoons dried oregano

1 teaspoon garlic powder

Crushed red pepper (optional)

SIRIOUSLY **SIMPLE**

Assemble the tortillas on a paper plate—this will help to easily slide them from the plate into the pan for cooking. To keep the pizzadillas hot during the cooking process, place them on a plate covered in foil until they are all done.

SIRIOUSLY **VARIED**

This recipe is so versatile, you can add any of your favorite pizza toppings to the mix: veggies, pepperoni, etc.

SIRIOUSLY **IMPORTANT**

Make sure you heat these on the stove with some butter—using a microwave won't produce the same crispy outer texture.

It's Five O'Clock Somewhere

Sing it with me! It's the most...wonderful tiiiiime...of the day. You know what I'm talking (or singing) about, and that is Happy Hour: that small stint of time when it is perfectly acceptable to sip an adult beverage while munching on a tasty snack. For its duration, life feels breezy and welcoming, with a hint of spontaneity. Of course, we've all heard the phrase "It's 5 o'clock somewhere," which essentially states that Happy Hour should not be confined to a specific time of day. I mean think about it, are we supposed to be miserable all other hours? I think not!

Therefore, I grant you permission to responsibly partake in these cocktails and appetizers whenever it pleases you—because you deserve it. Let me show you the way...

Imagine beginning a lazy Sunday morning with a sweet and spicy Bloody Mary and cheesy Spinach Balls before you feast on brunch, or kicking off a big game day with refreshing Transfusions and delicious Greek Nachos. Picture yourself mingling with friends during the holiday season, nibbling festive Rosemary Almonds and toasting frothy Brandy Alexanders. All of these scenarios demonstrate how "Happy Hour" is inherently a cheerful launching pad for even more joy. Honestly, whoever invented the appetizer is my hero (Let's eat food before we eat more food!). Of course, the most familiar time to engage in a happy hour episode is in the early evening, before your final meal of the day. Getting dinner ready can be a stressful time full of demanding, hungry bellies (your own included), and munching on hors d'oeuvres while sipping a libation can certainly take the edge off. A bubbly Mojito Mule and creamy Easy Edamame Hummus would be perfect for such an occasion. Also, sneaking words like "hors d'oeuvres" and "libation" into your vocabulary is life elevating, trust me.

In this happiest of chapters, you will find recipes for a delicious variety of finger foods and mixed drinks. The latter can be easily adapted into "mocktails" for kiddos or grown-ups not wishing to partake in alcohol. The appetizers range from light and nutritious to filling and slightly more indulgent, but they can all be easily whipped up in minimal time for any gathering. From seasoned Crispy Garbanzo Beans to peppery Cacio e Pepe Potato Chips, these recipes are uncomplicated, addictive and perfect for passing around. After all, Happy Hour should be shared, and sharing is caring. So grab your friends, grab a Spicy Grapefruit Cocktail and toast to 5 o'clock somewhere! Cheers!

½ cup Bloody Mary mix (such as Mr & Mrs T "Original")

6 tablespoons (3 ounces) vodka (such as Ketel One)

2 teaspoons Worcestershire sauce

½ tablespoon prepared horseradish

1 teaspoon bread-and-butter pickle juice (such as Bubbies)

1 teaspoon fresh lemon juice

3 dashes of hot sauce

Pinch of celery salt

Pinch of black pepper

Beef jerky

Lemon wedges

Celery stalks

Carson's Bloody Mary

You have no idea how coveted this recipe is. In fact, your cookbook might spontaneously combust after reading it. Sorry, you were warned. This particular Bloody Mary might be more famous than Carson (sorry, husband). He has all of these ingredients stocked at home, in his dressing room at the TODAY show, in his trailer at *The Voice*, in a Mary Poppins style handbag...okay that is fake news. The fact is this Bloody Mary is a highly requested beverage wherever he goes, and he has perfected it. While he can't quantify *exactly* how he makes it, I think I got pretty close with this recipe. The depth of flavor is highlighted from the smoky Worcestershire, the bright, fresh lemon, the sweet pickle juice and the spicy kick of hot sauce. Top with your favorite accoutrements like celery or beef jerky, and you have a meal in a glass. A famous one at that.

1   Fill a tall glass with lots of ice. Add the Bloody Mary mix, vodka, Worcestershire, horseradish, pickle juice, lemon juice, and hot sauce. Stir to combine.

2   Add more ice, if needed. Sprinkle with celery salt and pepper. If desired, garnish with beef jerky, lemon wedges, and celery stalks.

2 large white peaches, peeled and cut into thin wedges

1 cup halved seedless green grapes

1 cup halved seedless red grapes

2 cups chilled cantaloupe melon balls

1 (750-milliliter) bottle Moscato

½ cup peach nectar

¼ cup fresh lemon juice (from 2 lemons)

¼ cup (2 ounces) brandy

1 (12-ounce) can chilled peach-and-pear sparkling water

SIRIOUSLY MINI

Want to make smoothies for the kiddos? Process 1 peeled and chopped white peach, 1 cup cantaloupe melon balls, 1 cup frozen vanilla yogurt, ½ cup white seedless grapes, and ¼ cup peach nectar in a blender until smooth, about 30 seconds. Serve immediately.

Summer White Peach Sangria

Whenever I drink this, I like to pretend I'm sitting by the beach in Spain wearing a flowing dress, giant sunglasses and a big, floppy hat. In reality, of course, I'm in New York wearing a baseball cap and sweats, but this cocktail still has the power to make you feel as if you're on an endless vacation. While traditional sangria usually features red wine, this drink is made with a sweet white wine and accompanied by brandy and flavored sparkling water. There is nothing prettier than a rainbow of fruit swimming in a tall glass of alcohol, am I right? And because you can make it in a giant pitcher, it's the perfect beverage to serve a crowd at any gathering. They will be impressed, they will be refreshed, and they will feel as though you've whisked them away to a far-off place.

Place the peaches, grapes, and cantaloupe in a large pitcher or punchbowl. Add the Moscato, peach nectar, lemon juice, and brandy, and stir gently. Chill for 4 hours. When ready to serve, add the sparkling water, and serve chilled with plenty of fruit in each serving.

¼ cup (2 ounces) fresh grapefruit juice

¼ cup (2 ounces) silver tequila or vodka

2 tablespoons (1 ounce) orange liqueur (such as Cointreau)

2 serrano chile slices

SIRIOUSLY **SIMPLE**

For bigger quantities, pour into a closed pitcher with a lid, shake, and then pour over ice in glasses.

SIRIOUSLY **SPICY**

The longer the pepper sits in the cocktail, the spicier it will be. Remove the seeds for less heat.

Spicy Grapefruit Cocktail

Photograph on page 119

The first time I tried a cocktail like this, I was on a weekend "Fancy Camping" trip. If you have never "glamped," as it's often called, think basic camping with beds, showers, small fridges and WiFi. You're right, that's not like basic camping at all, but I swear it's fun. A friend made a batch of these spicy cocktails, and we have been making them ever since. Combining the sweet, tart grapefruit juice with the heat from the peppers creates such a refreshing beverage, with a kick. It's a visually appealing, delightful drink any time of year, but especially during those summer months when you're roughing it in the woods (with a bartender).

Stir together the juice, tequila, orange liqueur, and 1 serrano slice in a cocktail shaker with ice. Strain into a chilled martini glass. Garnish with the remaining serrano slice, if desired, and enjoy!

6 tablespoons ginger ale

¼ cup (2 ounces) vodka

¼ cup (2 ounces) grape juice

1 tablespoon fresh lemon juice

1 lemon wedge

SIRIOUSLY **SIMPLE**

Afraid of spilling grape juice on your carpet? Use white grape juice.

The Transfusion

Photograph on page 90

If a town has an official drink, then The Transfusion belongs to Manhasset, New York. Before moving to Long Island, I had never consumed the delightful mishmash of grape juice, ginger ale and vodka. Now it's become a staple beverage in our lives, like water or milk (I promise I drink more water than I do Transfusions, however). It's vibrant and sweet with a sparkling effervescence from the ginger ale. And did you know that grape juice has antioxidants and heart-friendly benefits, similar to red wine? It's true; I'm a doctor. You can't go wrong with this cocktail. Cheers!

Combine the ginger ale, vodka, grape juice, and lemon juice in a tall, ice-filled glass, and stir. Serve immediately with a lemon wedge.

Mojito Mule

Photograph on page 91

SERVES **1**
HANDS-ON TIME: **5 MINUTES**
TOTAL TIME: **5 MINUTES**

While Mojitos are super, and Moscow Mules are all fine and good, there is something extra special about the marriage of the two popular drinks. I introduce you to...the Mojito Mule—a refreshing beverage that combines the spicy fizz of a Moscow Mule with the sweet freshness of a Mojito. All of your friends will say, "Wow, you are uniquely creative when it comes to happy hour drinks." You may reply with, "Oh this old thing? All I did was muddle fresh mint and fresh lemon juice with tasty gin and a homemade simple syrup and topped it off with bubbly ginger beer." Be sure to serve it in a copper mug to really keep this crisp beverage icy and cool. It's the perfect drink marriage...I think it will last.

4 to 5 fresh mint leaves, plus more for garnish

2 tablespoons (1 ounce) dry gin

1 tablespoon fresh lemon juice

1 tablespoon Simple Syrup (recipe follows)

½ cup plus 2 tablespoons (5 ounces) ginger beer (such as Crabbie's Original Alcoholic Ginger Beer)

Lemon slice (optional)

Place the mint leaves, gin, lemon juice, and Simple Syrup in a copper mug. With a muddler or the handle of a wooden spoon, gently press the mint leaves to release oils. Add ice to the mug, and top with the ginger beer, stirring to blend the flavors. Serve immediately with a lemon slice, if desired.

Simple Syrup

MAKES **½ CUP**
HANDS-ON TIME: **5 MINUTES**
TOTAL TIME: **35 MINUTES**

Combine ½ cup granulated sugar and ½ cup water in a small saucepan over medium-high. Cook, stirring constantly, until the mixture simmers and the sugar dissolves, about 5 minutes. Remove from the heat, and cool completely, about 30 minutes.

SIRIOUSLY MINI

You can easily make this recipe into a mocktail for children or even adults who want to stay away from alcohol. Omit the gin, use nonalcoholic ginger beer, such as Ginger People Ginger Beer, and proceed with the above recipe as written.

The Transfusion
PG 88

Crispy
Garbanzo Beans
PG 96

Mojito Mule
PG 89

½ cup (4 ounces) brandy or cognac

¼ cup (2 ounces) dark crème de
cacao

½ cup plus 2 tablespoons heavy
cream

Pinch of freshly ground nutmeg

Brandy Alexander

Photograph on page 94

If you've ever lost a loved one, then you probably know that it never feels normal to refer to them in the past tense. My mother-in-law, Kiki, passed away in 2017, and the loss was monumental. I still struggle with writing as if she's gone, because her presence in my life is as strong today as it ever was. She was a woman deeply rooted in tradition. Every holiday has her stamp on it, from Halloween's "Goblin Goulash" to "Drunken Potatoes" at Thanksgiving to these Brandy Alexanders during Christmas time. Batch after batch would be blended up and served in the same red and green cups, year after year. To me, these signify the beginning of the holiday season. The frothy mixture is like a rich and creamy dessert in a glass. They are as festive as Kiki was, and serve as a gentle reminder of her beautiful spirit.

Combine the brandy, crème de cacao, and cream in a blender and process until very frothy, about 15 seconds. Pour into 2 chilled coupe glasses, and sprinkle with the freshly ground nutmeg. Serve immediately.

FOR A SINGLE SERVING, place ½ cup of ice in a cocktail shaker. Combine ¼ cup (2 ounces) of brandy or cognac, 2 tablespoons (1 ounce) of dark crème de cacao, and 5 tablespoons of heavy cream in the cocktail shaker; cover with the lid, and shake until very frothy, about 20 seconds. Strain into a chilled coupe glass, and sprinkle with freshly ground nutmeg.

The Dylan

Photograph on page 95

SERVES 1

HANDS-ON TIME: **10 MINUTES**
TOTAL TIME: **10 MINUTES**

This drink is named after my brother, Peter. Just kidding his name is Dylan! I am silly. My younger brother was a bartender for many years in Manhattan. While he's no longer in the service industry, he can still make a mean cocktail. In fact, Carson lovingly refers to him as a "drink snob" because while he's muddling, peeling, and shaking, we are simply opening a bottle of wine. This version of an Old Fashioned is his signature drink...sweet, citrusy whiskey that starts out slightly chilled and ends perfectly diluted. It's a classically smooth drink with a boozy, balanced finish. You don't have to be named Peter (or Dylan) to enjoy this cocktail.

1 to 2 Demerara sugar cubes

3 dashes of Angostura bitters

1 tablespoon club soda

¼ cup (2 ounces) rye whiskey

1 large ice cube

1 orange peel strip, white pith removed

1 lemon peel strip, white pith removed

Place the sugar cubes in an old fashioned glass. Add the bitters and club soda, and muddle with a spoon until the sugar dissolves. Add the rye whiskey and ice cube, and swirl the glass to combine the ingredients and chill the whiskey. Rub the rim of the glass with the orange and lemon strips; squeeze oils from both citrus strips over the mixture, and add the strips to the cocktail. Serve immediately.

"Peter" being snobby.

Brandy
Alexander
PG 92

The Dylan
PG 93

Rosemary
Almonds
PG 97

2 (15-ounce) cans chickpeas (garbanzo beans), drained and rinsed

2 tablespoons olive oil

1 tablespoon dried minced garlic

2 teaspoons ground cumin

1 ½ teaspoons kosher salt

⅛ teaspoon cayenne pepper

Crispy Garbanzo Beans

Photograph on page 90

Remember how I talked about how much I love the Crispy Garbanzo Beans from the Buddha Bowls in the Halftime chapter? Oh, you didn't realize I would quiz you in this cookbook to make sure you were paying attention? Well, you have no idea how bossy I was to my siblings when we used to play "teacher." (I was obviously *always* the teacher.) Alas, if you have forgotten, here is my reminder: I love these Crispy Garbanzo Beans! They are a nourishing, well-seasoned snack that will hook you at first bite. Seriously, I have been known to devour the entire batch. Luckily, they are rich in nutrients, therefore guilt-free. (Unless you are harboring guilt over failing my pop quiz, of course.) Make sure the beans are nice and dry before baking, which will add to the crispiness. Leaving them in the oven for a while also assists in getting that delicious crunch.

1 Preheat the oven to 350°F. Dry the chickpeas completely on paper towels. Arrange in a single layer on a rimmed baking sheet, and bake until completely dry, 4 to 5 minutes. (Do not turn off the oven.)

2 Stir together the olive oil, minced garlic, cumin, salt, and cayenne in a large bowl. Add the chickpeas; toss to coat. Spread the coated chickpeas on the baking sheet, return to the oven, and bake until dark brown, about 20 minutes, tossing occasionally.

3 Turn off the oven, and let the beans sit in the oven until crispy, about 45 minutes. Serve immediately or store in an airtight container at room temperature for up to 1 week.

Rosemary Almonds

Photograph on page 95

SERVES **8**
HANDS-ON TIME: **25 MINUTES**
TOTAL TIME: **25 MINUTES**

Back when I was a single, twentysomething living in Los Angeles, I would often frequent farmer's markets. There, I would casually stroll along, pretending I might buy a bunch of fresh fruits and vegetables to cook, fully knowing I would order takeout later on that night. It was a routine of sorts. However, one thing I could never pass up were the bags of flavored almonds. The only problem was I would usually empty out my wallet on them, as they were not cheap. It finally occurred to me I could make my own much more affordable version! These almonds are immensely flavorful with hints of sweetness, saltiness and spice all at once. It is a great recipe to double or triple for happy hour offerings, snacks on the go or even edible gifts without breaking the bank.

Preheat the oven to 350°F. Combine all of the ingredients in a bowl, and toss to coat. Spread the almonds in a single layer on a rimmed baking sheet. Bake until toasted, about 15 minutes, stirring twice during baking.

3 cups blanched almonds (about 15 ounces)

3 tablespoons olive oil

1 1/2 teaspoons lemon zest plus 1 tablespoon fresh juice

1 tablespoon chopped fresh rosemary

2 teaspoons honey

1 1/2 teaspoons kosher salt

3/4 teaspoon black pepper

1/2 teaspoon chili powder

SIRIOUSLY VARIED

Swap out the citrus—use orange or lime instead of the lemon—or the nut with cashews or peanuts.

SERVES **16**
HANDS-ON TIME: **15 MINUTES**
TOTAL TIME: **15 MINUTES**

1 cup popcorn kernels

½ cup plus 2 tablespoons Rosemary Infused Oil (recipe follows)

1 cup shredded Parmesan cheese

2 teaspoons kosher salt

Rosemary-Parmesan Popcorn

When my firstborn was little, we took him wherever we went. Work trips, vacations, fancy restaurants, even a happy hour jaunt once in awhile. One wintry day in New York City, we ducked into a bar with two-year-old Jack, had a beer, and munched on this flavorful popcorn. All three of us devoured it, and I happily knew it was something I could recreate at home. Popping popcorn on the stove is hands down my preferred cooking method, and in this instance the kernels are cooked in a super fragrant, rosemary-infused olive oil. The popular snack is elevated to a whole new level with the earthy, fresh herb and the salty Parmesan cheese. It's addictively delicious and a comforting recipe for all ages.

1 Stir the popcorn kernels and ½ cup of the oil in a large heavy saucepan over medium heat. Cover and cook until the kernels have popped, 8 to 9 minutes, shaking the pot halfway through cooking.

2 Immediately transfer the popcorn to a large bowl. Add the Parmesan, salt, and remaining 2 tablespoons of oil; toss to coat.

MAKES **2 CUPS**
HANDS ON TIME: **5 MINUTES**
TOTAL TIME: **20 MINUTES**

2 cups olive oil

4 fresh rosemary sprigs

Rosemary Infused Oil

1 Combine the oil and rosemary sprigs in a small heavy saucepan over medium. Cook until fragrant, about 5 minutes. Remove from the heat, and let cool to room temperature.

2 Place the rosemary sprigs in a 4-ounce bottle or cruet. Add the oil, and seal the lid. Use immediately or refrigerate for up to 1 month.

Cacio e Pepe Potato Chips

SERVES **6 TO 8**

HANDS-ON TIME: **5 MINUTES**

TOTAL TIME: **15 MINUTES**

I must admit something: I first shared this recipe on the TODAY show and immediately before the segment aired, I googled "how to pronounce Cacio e Pepe" and listened to the demonstration maybe 17 times in a row. If you are unfamiliar with the pronunciation, it goes something like this: "Couch-Oh EEE Pep-ay." I should probably translate professionally, huh? Anyways, Cacio e Pepe (meaning cheese and pepper) is one of my favorite Italian pasta dishes, so when I realized I could transform it into a chip it seemed like a no-brainer! This recipe is as simple as it gets, and it comes together in a matter of minutes. The chips are crispy and cheesy and peppery—all of the best things. Now go impress your friends with this effortless snack as well as your fancy Italian accent.

1 (8-ounce) package kettle-cooked potato chips

1 cup grated Parmigiano-Reggiano or Pecorino cheese

1 ½ teaspoons freshly ground black pepper

Chopped fresh parsley (optional)

1   Preheat the oven to 400°F. Arrange the potato chips in an even layer on a baking sheet lined with aluminum foil.

2   Sprinkle about half of the cheese on the chips, and bake until the cheese starts to melt, about 5 minutes.

3   Remove from the oven. Top with the remaining cheese, and sprinkle with the pepper. Let cool, scatter on some parsley if you'd like, and enjoy!

1/3 cup white miso

1 tablespoon rice vinegar

1 cup plain whole-milk Greek yogurt

1 (12-ounce) English cucumber, grated and squeezed dry

2 teaspoons grated fresh ginger

1 teaspoon kosher salt

1 garlic clove, minced

8 purple cauliflower florets

1 small yellow bell pepper, cut into strips

8 small radishes, quartered

1 cup sugar snap peas

3 medium carrots, peeled and cut into matchsticks

1/4 medium jicama, peeled and cut into matchsticks

SIRIOUSLY **FANCY**

Fill a shot glass with some of the dip and top with a few veggies for an easy-to-grab cocktail party appetizer.

Miso Tzatziki

When I was growing up, my mom always served us veggies and dip while she cooked dinner. Now that I'm a mother myself, I see the subtle brilliance in this. It kept our bellies satisfied without spoiling our appetites, and it held us close to the kitchen, happily munching away as she cooked. Her go-to was dill dip, which to this day tastes like my childhood, but I've grown to love many other kinds. While miso and tzatziki are two of my favorites, it occurred to me one day that the pair combined might be even better. Well guess what, it is! It is thick and creamy with essences of sweet, salty and umami flavors. Make sure to squeeze the excess water out of the grated cucumber to prevent a runny dip. Hungry bellies before dinner, be gone!

Place the miso, vinegar, and 2 tablespoons of the yogurt in a bowl. Whisk vigorously until smooth. Add the cucumber, ginger, salt, garlic, and remaining yogurt; whisk until smooth. Serve with the veggies.

1 pound smoked whitefish or trout

5 hard-cooked egg whites

1 small white onion, chopped

1 ½ cups mayonnaise

3 tablespoons fresh lemon juice

2 tablespoons minced fresh chives,
plus more for garnish

½ teaspoon kosher salt

½ teaspoon freshly ground black
pepper

Saltine crackers

Hot sauce

SIRIOUSLY **SIMPLE**

Use the leftover egg yolks in a
homemade egg salad.

Smoked Whitefish Dip

Photograph on page 106

This dip is directly inspired by something served at one of my
favorite L.A. restaurants, Son of a Gun. The chefs and owners, Jon
Shook and Vinny Dotolo, were the very first guests that I worked
with back in my segment-producing days at *Last Call with Carson
Daly*. At that point, they were just opening their first restaurant, and
now they have multiple award-winning hot spots in the L.A. area. It
makes me feel very old to use the phrase, "I knew them when…" but
hey, I guess I am very old. This whitefish dip is superb on so many
levels, primarily because of the smoky flavor, creamy texture and the
crispy, salty vessel it's served on. Please, only use saltine crackers.
There is something very necessary about them, as well as the dash
of hot sauce atop each bite. If you ever get the chance to dine at
Son of a Gun, do that, but in the meantime make this delicious dip
and pretend you are a celebrity chef.

Pulse the whitefish in a food processor until finely chopped, 6 to 8 times;
transfer to a bowl. Pulse the egg whites in a food processor until finely
chopped, 6 to 8 times; add to the fish. Repeat the process with the onion.
Stir in the mayonnaise, lemon juice, chives, salt, and pepper. Sprinkle with
extra chives and serve immediately with the crackers and hot sauce, or
refrigerate until ready to serve (up to 1 week).

Vinny

Jon

Easy Edamame Hummus

Photograph on page 107

MAKES **4 CUPS**
HANDS-ON TIME: **5 MINUTES**
TOTAL TIME: **5 MINUTES**

1 (16-ounce) container hummus

**2 cups shelled frozen edamame,
thawed, plus a handful for garnish**

3 tablespoons fresh lemon juice

**2 tablespoons extra-virgin olive oil,
plus more for drizzling**

1 teaspoon sea salt

**1/2 teaspoon freshly ground black
pepper**

I am all about a semi-homemade recipe. Shortcuts are often essential in life, and that applies to cooking as well. We are all busy people. At any given moment, like right now as you're reading this, you might be able to list five other things you could (should?) be doing. Perhaps you think whipping up a nutritious and delicious snack is not a priority? WRONG. I'm here to rudely tell you that you're wrong. One of my favorite shortcuts is taking something store-bought, like hummus in this instance, and doctoring it up. It's the quickest way to make an easy appetizer that looks and tastes time consuming. Here, buttery edamame beans are blended with premade hummus, fresh lemon juice and good olive oil to create a smooth, creamy and perfectly balanced dip. Go ahead and claim you were up all night making it, I won't tell.

Combine the hummus, edamame, lemon juice, oil, salt, and pepper in a food processor, and process until smooth, about 10 seconds. Transfer to a serving bowl, drizzle with the olive oil, and sprinkle over a few more edamame.

Smoked
Whitefish Dip
PG 104

Easy Edamame
Hummus
PG 105

Greek Nachos

SERVES **8**
HANDS-ON TIME: **20 MINUTES**
TOTAL TIME: **35 MINUTES**

If you make anything from this cookbook, make these Greek Nachos. Right now. Stop everything you're doing, go buy these ingredients, and make. these. nachos. As you can tell, I am very passionate about how good they are. Not good, outstanding. Epic. I could keep listing synonyms for "tremendous" from the thesaurus, if you'd like? But I won't, because I know you will agree with me. First, bake up perfectly seasoned, homemade pita chips, top them with creamy crumbled feta cheese, chopped veggies, and salty olives and finally drizzle everything with a spicy yogurt sauce. Then, come back to this page and nod in agreement with the magic that is this recipe. Each ingredient merged together creates a unified, delightful appetizer that will make any happy hour even happier.

1   **Make the Dressing:** Whisk together all of the ingredients until smooth.

2   **Make the Nachos:** Preheat the oven to 400°F. Cut each pita into 8 wedges. Arrange the pita wedges in a single layer on an aluminum foil-lined rimmed baking sheet. Brush the pita wedges with the oil, and sprinkle with the paprika and salt. Bake until crisp, 10 to 12 minutes.

3   Remove the pita wedges from the oven. Increase the heat to a high broil. Sprinkle the wedges with the feta, bell pepper, and red onion. Broil until the cheese starts to melt, about 3 minutes. Remove from the oven.

4   Sprinkle with the tomato, olives, and chives. Transfer the dressing to a squeeze bottle, or spoon into a plastic ziplock bag and snip 1 corner to make a small hole. Drizzle the nachos with your desired amount of dressing. Reserve any remaining dressing for another use.

DRESSING

1 cup plain whole-milk Greek yogurt

3 tablespoons fresh lemon juice

1 tablespoon honey

1 teaspoon garlic powder

¼ teaspoon cayenne pepper

NACHOS

6 (5-inch) pita rounds

3 tablespoons olive oil

1½ teaspoons paprika

1 teaspoon kosher salt

1½ cups crumbled feta cheese

1 large red bell pepper, chopped

1 medium-sized red onion, finely chopped

1 medium tomato, chopped

¾ cup sliced kalamata olives

3 tablespoons thinly sliced fresh chives

SIRIOUSLY MINI

To make this more kid-friendly, top the toasted pita with store-bought hummus, feta, and diced avocado.

BBQ Chicken Nacho Bites

This recipe was created for a cowboy. That's right, these nacho bites were inspired by the one and only Blake Shelton (the only cowboy I know). At the time, I was working on a "*Voice* Tailgate" series for my blog, cultivating dishes that reflected each coach's personal and musical style. To me, Blake is sweet, but with a tangy kick. (I don't really know how that translates—let's just go with "he's sarcastic.") And cowboys like BBQ, right? (I realize that's stereotypical, and Blake's favorite thing to eat is calamari, so...) Regardless, these BBQ Chicken Nacho Bites are the perfect tailgate snack. They are alarmingly easy to make and addictively easy to eat. Your friends, your kids and your cowboys will gobble them up.

4 (10-inch) flour tortillas

Cooking spray

2 (6-ounce) cooked boneless, skinless chicken breasts, shredded

½ cup barbecue sauce

1 cup preshredded Mexican cheese blend

½ cup diced tomato

¼ cup sliced pitted black olives

2 tablespoons chopped fresh cilantro

1   Preheat the oven to 350°F. Using a 3-inch round cookie cutter (or a glass similar in size), cut 3 circles out of each tortilla.

2   Spray a 12-cup muffin pan with cooking spray. Press the tortilla rounds into the muffin pan cups to create small bowls. Spray the top of each tortilla with cooking spray.

3   Bake until slightly golden around the edges, about 14 minutes. Remove from the oven, and increase the heat to 400°F.

4   Stir together the shredded chicken and barbecue sauce in a small bowl. Place about ¼ cup of the chicken mixture into each tortilla bowl and sprinkle evenly with the shredded cheese. Bake until the cheese is melted and bubbly, 8 to 10 minutes.

5   Carefully remove the tortilla bowls from the muffin pan. Top evenly with the tomatoes, olives, and cilantro.

SIRIOUSLY SPICY

Kick the heat up a notch by adding sliced jalapeños to these!

Borrowing the Cowboy's Chair.

Spinach Balls

Imagine the most delicious spinach dip you've ever eaten...in ball form. That's a weird way to describe this appetizer. These cheesy Spinach Balls are as decadent as a rich and creamy dip, but without all the heavy, thick cheese. They are formed into "pop-in-your-mouth" bites that make them the perfect party recipe. Trust me, even those little people who fear "green things" (my children) will crave this snack. Especially if you can convince them to assist in rolling out each small ball with their helpful little hands. Working with kids in the kitchen usually translates to more flexible palates. USUALLY. I am not promising miracles here. What I am promising is a simple, tasty recipe that you will want to make again and again.

1 Preheat the oven to 350°F. Stir together the spinach, breadcrumbs, onion, butter, Parmesan, salt, pepper, and eggs in a large bowl until combined. Measuring 1 tablespoon at a time, roll the mixture into 48 balls, and place them on a greased baking sheet.

2 Bake until the edges are golden, about 30 minutes, rotating the baking sheet halfway through cooking.

MAKES **48**
HANDS ON TIME: **15 MINUTES**
TOTAL TIME: **45 MINUTES**

2 (10-ounce) packages frozen chopped spinach, thawed, drained, and squeezed of all moisture

2 cups Italian-seasoned breadcrumbs

1 yellow onion, diced

3/4 cup unsalted butter, melted

1/2 cup grated Parmesan cheese

1 teaspoon kosher salt

1/2 teaspoon freshly ground black pepper

4 large eggs

SIRIOUSLY IMPORTANT
Be sure that you squeeze all the moisture out of the thawed spinach to avoid soggy balls (sorry!).

1 (8-ounce) French baguette, cut
  diagonally into 16 slices

¼ cup extra-virgin olive oil, plus
  more for garnish

8 ounces burrata cheese, drained

2 large white peaches, thinly sliced

¼ cup sliced fresh basil

2 tablespoons honey

1 teaspoon coarse sea salt

Burrata and White Peach Crostini

If summer could be served on toast, it would want to be served on this crostini. What else personifies those hot, mid-year months more than perfectly ripe peaches paired with luscious burrata cheese? No school, lazy long days, mosquitos...okay fine, they scream SUMMER as well. However, I only speak food. This appetizer is meant to be enjoyed on your porch, in a rocking chair, with a glass of pink wine. If you're unable to make that happen, you will still adore this sweet and salty toast. The fusion of flavors and textures will make your palate relaxed and happy. Summer is a state of mind, after all, and food is a gateway to such disposition. Deep Thoughts, by Siri Daly.

1   Preheat the oven to 400°F. Brush both sides of the bread slices with the olive oil, and place on a baking sheet. Bake until golden brown, about 12 minutes, turning halfway through.

2   Spread 2 teaspoons of the burrata on each toast. Top evenly with the peach slices and basil. Drizzle with the honey, and sprinkle with the coarse sea salt. Garnish with a drizzle of olive oil, if desired.

2 cups diced fresh butternut squash

2 tablespoons olive oil

1/2 teaspoon freshly ground black pepper

1 1/2 teaspoons kosher salt

1 (12-ounce) French baguette, cut into 24 slices

2 tablespoons unsalted butter

1 leek, sliced

1 1/2 cups ricotta cheese

1 1/2 tablespoons balsamic glaze

1 teaspoon coarse sea salt (optional)

Butternut Squash, Leek, and Ricotta Toast

Photograph on page 118

Were we just talking about summer? Summer shmummer. Fall is where it's at! Butternut squash is one of my favorite vegetables to cook when the weather turns cooler. There are many ways to prepare it, but roasting is my favorite. Notably, when one is roasting in your oven, the sweet and nutty aromas that emanate scream autumn. Once the pumpkin-like squash is cooked, I love to pair it with creamy ricotta and caramelized leeks and serve the combination on crusty toast. Drizzled with thick, balsamic glaze for a little edge, this satisfyingly rich appetizer will certainly please all. As well as please fall. (See what I did there?!)

1   Preheat the oven to 400°F. Place the squash on a baking sheet, drizzle with the olive oil, and sprinkle with the pepper and 1 teaspoon of the kosher salt. Toss to coat, and spread in an even layer.

2   Place the bread slices on another baking sheet. Place both baking sheets in the oven and bake until the bread is browned, about 10 minutes, and the squash is caramelized and tender, 13 to 15 minutes.

3   Meanwhile, melt the butter in a small skillet over medium. Add the sliced leek and remaining 1/2 teaspoon kosher salt. Cook, stirring often, until the leek begins to caramelize, 8 to 10 minutes.

4   To assemble the toasts, spread 2 teaspoons of the ricotta on each toast. Top evenly with the leeks and butternut squash, drizzle with the balsamic glaze, and, if desired, sprinkle with sea salt.

Smashed Pea and Ricotta Toast

Photograph on page 119

SERVES **12**

HANDS-ON TIME: **25 MINUTES**

TOTAL TIME: **25 MINUTES**

If you're not a fan of peas, come closer and let me tell you something: You've probably been eating them all wrong! Mushy, bland peas are of yesteryear...today they are fresh, vibrant and wonderful. While I appreciate crisp, buttery peas in their simplest form, something tremendous happens when they are pureed into a chunky, pesto-like spread as they are here. The smashed consistency is ideal with the other textures involved, like creamy ricotta and crusty bread. Combined, it is subtly sweet, mostly savory and entirely flavorful. The flecks of red pepper add a nice kick of heat, as well as a visual contrast to the bright green peas. This is the perfect appetizer to pass around at any gathering!

1 (12-ounce) French baguette, cut into 24 slices

7 tablespoons olive oil

2 cups frozen sweet peas, thawed

¼ cup chopped fresh basil leaves, plus more for garnish

1 teaspoon kosher salt

½ teaspoon freshly ground black pepper

1 garlic clove, roughly chopped

2 cups ricotta cheese

1 ½ teaspoons honey

1 ½ teaspoons crushed red pepper (optional)

1 Preheat the oven to 400°F. Place the baguette slices on a baking sheet, and evenly brush the slices with 3 tablespoons of the olive oil. Bake until golden brown, about 10 minutes, turning halfway through. Transfer to a platter.

2 Fill a medium saucepan half full with water, and bring to a boil over medium-high. Prepare a bowl of ice water. Add the peas to the boiling water, and cook for 2 minutes. Drain and immediately place the peas in the ice water. Let stand for 3 minutes, then drain.

3 Process the peas, basil, salt, pepper, garlic and 3 tablespoons of the olive oil in a blender or food processor until the peas reach a smashed consistency, about 5 seconds.

4 Stir together the ricotta and honey in a small bowl.

5 Assemble the toasts by spreading 2 teaspoons of the ricotta mixture on each slice, and top with 1 teaspoon of the pea mixture. Evenly drizzle the remaining 1 tablespoon oil on the toasts. Sprinkle with basil and, if desired, crushed red pepper.

SIRIOUSLY SIMPLE

Blanching the peas and placing them in a bowl of ice water after boiling prevents them from cooking further and preserves their bright green color. If you're not a fan of peas, your favorite store-bought pesto would work well as a replacement.

Butternut Squash, Leek,
and Ricotta Toast
PG 116

Smashed Pea and
Ricotta Toast
PG 117

Spicy Grapefruit
Cocktail
PG 88

FOUR

Time for Dinner

I've always had a fantasy of living on a vast ranch, where my children roam with horses and frolic in meadows, and when it comes time for dinner, I ring a giant cowbell to summon them home. We sit together at a wide table, passing around family-style dishes, happily chatting about our pleasant days. Sounds idyllic, right? In reality, I'm yelling at them from the next room to please come eat before we have to move on to homework, baths, bedtimes, and the like. While dinner in my house is rarely leisurely, it is important. Eating together as a family was something both Carson and I did growing up, so we try to prioritize that with our kids. There might not be horses or cowbells, but it is a time for us to check in with each other over a shared meal.

Now when I say, "shared meal," does that mean we are all eating the exact same thing every night? Not always (cue: eye roll). However, I try my best to make one dish that can accommodate various taste buds. Adaptable recipes have always topped my list of dinner priorities. Other criteria on that list include balanced options and approachable recipes. Let's start with balance—the secret to a happy life. To me, the key to maintaining healthy behavior is to embrace a kind of harmony when it comes to food. That means, if you eat Fried Chicken one night, stick to Grilled Swordfish with Crispy Capers the next. It's all about proportion, and evening things out. I've never believed that depriving yourself entirely of something is productive. Life is too short not to indulge every once in awhile!

Now for those approachable recipes, because, let's face it, dinner can be a hectic time of day. Maybe you've just come home from work, your kids from school or activities (and they're "starving!"—another eye roll), maybe you have no idea what to eat, or feel like you have nothing in your fridge... whatever the reason, it's never easy to prepare a meal when you're feeling rushed or uninspired. Therefore, I like to have recipes in my back pocket that I can rely on for simplicity and time-management and that require minimal ingredients. With meals like Sneaky One-Pot Mexican Pasta that's made in one pot or Quick Chicken Masala that comes together in under thirty minutes, dinner doesn't have to feel like an impossible feat to pull off.

Let's finish where we started with adaptable meals. I'm not just talking about recipes that can be modified for picky eaters—although those do exist in this chapter (see: Crispy Chicken Paillard). I'm referring to dinners where ingredients can be swapped, omitted or added, depending on preference or what you have to work with. Adaptable dinners are also crucial for a big group of people...meals like Slow-Cooked Pulled Pork Chalupas or Loaded Baked Potatoes are ideal for a crowd because they can be easily customized.

However your day unfolds—whether you feel fried or relaxed by the end of it—dinner is the meal that wraps everything up and gives us the fuel we need to take on another day. You ought to treat it right!

Arugula Pesto Bow-Tie Pasta

1 pound uncooked farfalle (bow-tie) pasta

½ cup pine nuts

¼ cup grated Parmesan cheese, plus shaved cheese for topping

1 garlic clove, roughly chopped

2 cups loosely packed baby arugula

½ cup extra-virgin olive oil

1 ½ teaspoons sea salt

1 cup sun-dried tomatoes in oil, drained and thinly sliced

SIRIOUSLY **VARIED**

Since pine nuts can sometimes cost one billion dollars, try using almonds instead to save some money!

Pesto is one of the first things I taught myself to make. Essentially, it's a very simple sauce made with minimal ingredients, but it feels like much more than that. First, it's visually stunning with its vibrant green color...almost too pretty to eat! (Almost.) Second, it's very versatile. A traditional pesto is made with basil, but in this recipe I use peppery arugula to mix it up (you can also try kale or spinach). Finally, there's something about quickly whipping up a homemade sauce that is very ego boosting, and isn't that an important part of cooking? It makes me feel like a professional, fancy chef when I'm basically doing something extremely easy. Pesto for the win! I often make a double batch, freezing half and serving the rest on top of yummy bow-tie pasta with sun-dried tomatoes. Just make sure to save the leftovers, because it's even better the next day.

1   Bring a large saucepan of water to a boil. Add a generous amount of salt, then your pasta, and cook according to the package instructions; drain.

2   Meanwhile make your pesto: Place the pine nuts in a dry skillet over medium, and cook, stirring constantly to prevent burning, until they just begin to brown, 2 to 3 minutes. Remove from the skillet, and let cool.

3   Combine the Parmesan, garlic, and half of the pine nuts in a food processor or blender. Pulse until finely ground. Add the arugula and process, slowly pouring in the olive oil through the food chute, until desired consistency is reached. Stir in ½ teaspoon of the salt.

4   Return the drained pasta back to the saucepan. Stir in the pesto and sun-dried tomatoes. Sprinkle with the remaining 1 teaspoon salt. Divide the pasta evenly among 6 bowls, and top with the remaining pine nuts and shaved Parmesan.

Slow-Cooker Mac and Cheese

My Crock-Pot is like a member of my family. I've never named it, but I'm going to now. Chester. Chester, the Crock-Pot. Chester is very loyal and always comes through for me (which is the definition of loyal), especially when it comes to this Slow-Cooker Mac and Cheese. It is delightfully creamy, hearty and completely uncomplicated. No need to stand over a hot stove, whisking away at a roux until it forms a thickened sauce. Instead, it's as simple as tossing everything in a Crock-Pot and letting Chester do the rest! I won't lie to you...I break out the boxed mac and cheese more than I'd like to admit. However, if you plan ahead—just a tiny bit—then you can easily whip up this decadent, homemade version in no time. Most importantly, it is children-who-love-the-boxed-version approved, and because it's so simple to make (thanks, Chester), it will fit nicely into any weeknight dinner plan.

1 Bring the water to a boil in a large saucepan. Add the pasta, and cook for 6 minutes (the pasta will not be tender). Drain, and rinse with cold water; drain again.

2 Combine the butter, flour, and salt in a 4-quart slow cooker, stirring with a whisk. Stir in the half-and-half, mozzarella, and ½ cup of the Cheddar. Add the partially cooked pasta, stirring to coat. Cover and cook on LOW until slightly thickened and creamy, about 1 ½ hours. Remove the lid, stir, and sprinkle with the remaining 1 cup Cheddar. Cover and cook until the cheese is melted and the liquid is nearly absorbed, 15 to 30 minutes.

SERVES **6**
HANDS-ON TIME: **25 MINUTES**
TOTAL TIME: **2 HOURS 15 MINUTES**

8 cups water

12 ounces uncooked large elbow macaroni

¼ cup unsalted butter, melted

1 tablespoon all-purpose flour

1 ½ teaspoons kosher salt

3 cups half-and-half

1 ½ cups preshredded mozzarella cheese

1 ½ cups preshredded Cheddar cheese

SIRIOUSLY **FANCY**

Stir in 1 (16-ounce) package diced ham and 2 cups frozen, thawed green peas before sprinkling with the remaining 1 cup Cheddar.

SIRIOUSLY **IMPORTANT**

Partially precooking the macaroni ensures that it is all the way cooked through but not too soft.

2 cups cooked white rice

2 cups finely diced broccoli florets

1 cup frozen sweet peas, thawed

1 (13.5-ounce) can coconut milk, well shaken

½ cup cream cheese, softened

1 teaspoon kosher salt

½ teaspoon black pepper

1 cup grated Cheddar cheese

SIRIOUSLY VARIED

Along (or in place of) the diced broccoli and peas, you could really throw anything in here: cubed ham, bell peppers, onions, chicken, etc., whatever you're in the mood for or have on hand!

Cheesy Green Rice Casserole

Photograph on page 131

For a short time in my twenties, I lived with my younger sister, and we ate chicken and rice almost every night for dinner. Sometimes we got fancy and threw in onions or green bell peppers, and there was always Cheddar cheese on top. We would start with a small helping, and then we would go back for more, and more and more, because we are sisters, and we are the same. We usually drank Bacardi and Diet Coke as well, and we watched stupid television. I can actually taste all of this as I type...especially the rum. Anyway, this cheesy casserole reminds me a little of our chicken and rice nights, perhaps because it is very simple to make, or maybe because it is comfort food at its best. All I know is that I love it, and it's a great way to sneak some veggies into your diet. The coconut milk gives it a subtle, tropical flair, which makes it all the more appealing for cozy, cold nights at home. Make this with your sissy, and serve it with rum and stupid TV.

1 Preheat the oven to 400°F.

2 Stir together the rice, broccoli, peas, coconut milk, cream cheese, salt, and pepper in a large bowl.

3 Spoon the mixture into a lightly greased 13- x 9-inch baking dish. Sprinkle with the grated Cheddar.

4 Bake until the cheese is bubbly and golden, 15 to 20 minutes.

Southwest Spaghetti Squash

Photograph on page 130

I am a huge fan of Southwestern flavors like cumin, cilantro, scallions, CHEESE...which is why I love this dinner so much. It has all the elements of a rich, hearty Southwestern meal, but tastes and feels much lighter thanks to the spaghetti squash base. My sister-in-law first made something like this, and I felt inspired. I should mention—she is very inspiring when it comes to healthful, nutritious, yet tasty meals. That is why on her birthday every year, I make her eat a dozen donuts, which is another story for another time. Back to this flavorful dish...it makes a perfect vegetarian meal with an added protein boost from the black beans, and anything with melted, bubbly cheese on top is appealing to most anyone, especially kiddos. Just make sure your knife is sharp when you cut the squash in half, or, ask your sister-in-law to do it, because she works out way more than you do...

1 Preheat the oven to 350°F.

2 Coat an 11- x 7-inch baking dish with cooking spray. Place the squash, cut side down, in the baking dish, and bake until tender, about 45 minutes. Let squash cool slightly but keep oven on.

3 Scrape the inside of the squash with a fork to remove the spaghetti-like strands, and place them in a bowl.

4 Add the tomatoes, beans, scallions, cilantro, cumin, garlic salt, kosher salt, pepper, and ½ cup of the cheese. If desired, sprinkle with hot sauce, and stir.

5 Transfer back to the baking dish, and top with the remaining ½ cup cheese.

6 Bake until the top is bubbly and the cheese is melted, about 30 minutes. Serve immediately. If you want, garnish with cilantro, and serve with sour cream.

SERVES **6**
HANDS-ON TIME: **25 MINUTES**
TOTAL TIME: **1 HOUR 40 MINUTES**

Cooking spray

1 spaghetti squash, sliced lengthwise, seeds removed

1 (14-ounce) can diced tomatoes and green bell peppers, drained

1 (14-ounce) can black beans, drained and rinsed

1 bunch scallions, white and pale green parts only, finely chopped

¼ cup finely chopped fresh cilantro, plus more for garnish

1 teaspoon ground cumin

½ teaspoon garlic salt

½ teaspoon kosher salt

¼ teaspoon black pepper

1 cup shredded Monterey Jack (or Mexican cheese blend)

Dash of hot sauce (optional)

Sour cream (optional)

Southwest
Spaghetti Squash
PG 129

Cheesy Green
Rice Casserole
PG 128

SERVES **6**
HANDS-ON TIME: **15 MINUTES**
TOTAL TIME: **1 HOUR**
10 MINUTES

1 ½ cups sliced zucchini (from 1 zucchini)

1 ½ cups cherry tomatoes

1 cup chopped yellow bell pepper (from 1 bell pepper)

1 cup sliced red onion (from 1 small onion)

3 tablespoons olive oil

1 ½ teaspoons kosher salt

½ teaspoon black pepper

12 ounces uncooked spaghetti

1 cup half-and-half

3 large eggs, lightly beaten

1 cup grated Parmesan cheese

1 cup preshredded mozzarella cheese

Chopped fresh parsley

Spaghetti Primavera Pie

Pasta transformed into pie...is there anything more that needs to be said to describe the brilliance of this dish? Okay fine, I'll keep going. Imagine spaghetti, boiled until al dente, mixed together with well-seasoned, roasted-until-tender vegetables, tossed in a creamy, cheesy sauce, topped with even more cheese (obviously) and baked until bubbly, golden and perfectly set. Now imagine that in your mouth...or, instead of daydreaming until you salivate, make it for dinner tonight! Nothing about this dish is difficult; rather, it's surprisingly effortless. You likely have most of these ingredients and if you don't, the vegetables are completely interchangeable—asparagus, yellow squash or mushrooms would be lovely swaps or additions. If you, or any smaller humans in your life, are struggling to get enough veggies in your diet, this is a creative way to work them in. It's spaghetti, after all, in deep-dish pie form, and as I mentioned earlier...enough said.

1   Preheat the oven to 400°F. Place the zucchini, tomatoes, bell pepper, and red onion on a rimmed baking sheet. Drizzle with the oil, and sprinkle with ½ teaspoon of the salt and ¼ teaspoon of the black pepper; toss to coat evenly. Bake until the vegetables are tender and lightly browned, stirring once, about 20 minutes. Keep oven on.

2   Meanwhile, cook the pasta according to the package directions for al dente; drain.

3   Whisk together the half-and-half, eggs, and remaining 1 teaspoon salt and ¼ teaspoon black pepper in a medium bowl. Add the cooked pasta and ½ cup each of the Parmesan and mozzarella, tossing to coat. Add the vegetables, and toss gently. Transfer to a lightly greased 9 ½-inch deep-dish pie pan. Sprinkle with the remaining ½ cup each Parmesan and mozzarella. Bake until set and cheese has browned, about 30 minutes. Remove from the oven, and let stand 5 to 10 minutes before serving. Garnish with parsley.

Loaded Baked Potato Bar

SERVES 8

HANDS-ON TIME: **15 MINUTES**

TOTAL TIME: **1 HOUR 30 MINUTES**

When I was pregnant with my son, Jackson, I craved baked potatoes, all of the time. Well, that's not entirely true, I also craved applesauce mixed together with cottage cheese, but you don't really need a recipe for that yummy (weird) combo. Quite honestly, you barely need a recipe for these scrumptiously loaded-up taters, either! It's as simple as brushing some Yukon Golds all over with oil, generously seasoning them with salt and pepper and baking them for about an hour so that you're left with a crispy skin and a light, fluffy interior. After that, it's all about creating your own culinary masterpiece with various toppings, my favorites being smoky chicken, crispy bacon, juicy tomatoes and fresh cilantro. Oh, and cheese because, always cheese. The more you pile on, the heartier the meal. This is a really fun dinner to serve at a casual gathering because everyone can customize their own plate. Which also makes it ideal for those nights when your family can't decide on one thing—not that that EVER happens to me...

- 8 (6-ounce) Yukon Gold potatoes or sweet potatoes
- 1 tablespoon olive oil
- 1 teaspoon kosher salt
- ½ teaspoon black pepper
- 2 cups shredded skinless rotisserie chicken breast
- 6 to 8 bacon slices, cooked and crumbled
- ½ cup chopped plum tomato
- 1 cup shredded Monterey Jack cheese, or any other melty cheese
- Sour cream (optional)
- Chopped fresh cilantro (optional)
- Diced jalapeño chile (optional)
- Hot sauce (optional)

1 Preheat the oven to 375°F. Pierce the potatoes all over with a fork, and rub with the oil. Place the potatoes on a rimmed baking sheet, and sprinkle with the salt and pepper. Bake until very tender, about 1 hour. Remove from the oven, and let stand about 10 minutes, but keep the oven on.

2 Slice each potato to, but not through, the other side. Gently open the potatoes, and flake the potato pulp with a fork. Top each potato evenly with the chicken, bacon, tomato, and cheese. Return the potatoes to the baking sheet, and bake until the cheese is melted, about 5 minutes. Serve with sour cream, cilantro, jalapeño, and hot sauce, if desired.

¼ cup unsalted butter

½ cup hot sauce (such as Tabasco)

1 pound ground chicken

1 cup panko (Japanese-style breadcrumbs)

½ small yellow onion, finely diced

2 celery stalks, finely diced

1 large egg, lightly beaten

1 teaspoon kosher salt

½ teaspoon garlic powder

½ cup plain whole-milk Greek yogurt

¼ cup crumbled blue cheese

Chopped fresh parsley

SIRIOUSLY IMPORTANT

You want to get the meatballs slightly crispy on the outside, so leave them in the oven until you can see or feel that the exterior is turning brown. Then toss them in the sauce and serve immediately.

Buffalo Chicken Meatballs

You know that song that goes, "Oh give me a home, where the buffalo roam,"—they're referring to buffalo hot sauce, right? Wrong? Golly, well then, what a silly, classic, time-honored, distinguished American song. I might have to write my own tune about the famous condiment because, as you can see, I am a huge fan. The wonderfully spicy, smooth, buttery sauce has enough tinge of sweetness to balance everything out so yes, I love buffalo-flavored ANYTHING, and these meatballs do not disappoint. They are baked, therefore much healthier than their cousin, the buffalo chicken wing, but still maintain a slightly crisp exterior without needing to be fried. Of course, anything with heat needs a cooling down factor, and this Greek-yogurt-based blue cheese sauce completes the dish in that manner. I would serve this with a big green salad and a side of home, home on the range.

1 Preheat the oven to 400°F. Melt the butter with the hot sauce in a small saucepan over medium. Whisk until combined; remove from heat, and let cool about 5 minutes.

2 Stir together the ground chicken, panko, onion, celery, egg, salt, garlic powder, and half of the hot sauce mixture until combined. Set the remaining hot sauce mixture aside.

3 Shape the chicken mixture into 30 meatballs, and place on a parchment paper-lined baking sheet. Bake the meatballs until a meat thermometer registers 165°F, 15 to 18 minutes, rotating the pan halfway through cooking time. Increase the oven temperature to high broil without removing the pan. Broil the meatballs until golden brown and crispy, 3 to 5 minutes. Remove from the oven, and toss with the remaining hot sauce mixture in a bowl.

4 Stir together the Greek yogurt and blue cheese. Serve the meatballs immediately with the blue cheese–yogurt sauce and sprinkled with the parsley.

Spicy Sweet
Potato Rounds
PG 184

Daly Fried Chicken

Carson's mother—Kiki, as the grandkids called her—was an army brat and grew up all over the world, but her roots were in North Carolina. She would tell countless stories about her childhood, recalling the days on her grandmother's farm and the family-style dinners with proper Southern cuisine. One summer, she and I saw *The Help*, a film set in the South, and she left feeling inspired to cook legitimate soul food, more specifically, fried chicken. (I left with a swollen face from "ugly crying" but that's neither here nor there.) Up until that day, I had never experienced this acclaimed meal but after, I would beg her to make it again and again. I am so thankful she shared her recipes with me, because even though she is no longer physically with us, her spirit lives on in measureless ways. When we eat this crispy, juicy fried chicken served with mashed potatoes and braised greens (or in my version, Spicy Sweet Potato Rounds) it feels like she's sitting at the table with us. Food such as this is made with love, and that will endure the test of time.

1 In a large baking dish, soak the chicken in the buttermilk, preferably overnight (or for as long as possible).

2 When ready to fry, set up a station near the stove: Whisk together the eggs, 1 teaspoon of the salt, and ½ teaspoon of the pepper in a shallow dish. Whisk together the flour and remaining 1 teaspoon salt and ½ teaspoon pepper in another shallow dish.

3 Melt enough vegetable shortening in a cast-iron skillet over medium-high until the melted shortening is about 1 inch deep in the skillet. Heat the oil to 325°F.

4 Remove the chicken from the buttermilk, allowing most of the buttermilk to drip back into the bowl. Dredge in the flour mixture; dip in the egg mixture, and dredge again in the flour mixture.

5 Carefully place the chicken in the hot oil in the skillet, and fry until golden and cooked through with an internal temperature of about 170°F, about 15 minutes, turning halfway through cooking time. Remove the chicken, and place on a baking sheet lined with paper towels to drain.

SERVES **6**

HANDS-ON TIME: **30 MINUTES**

TOTAL TIME: **8 HOURS 30 MINUTES**

2 ½ pounds dark meat chicken pieces

1 quart whole buttermilk

5 large eggs

2 teaspoons kosher salt

1 teaspoon black pepper

4 cups all-purpose flour

Vegetable shortening

SIRIOUSLY IMPORTANT

Make sure to monitor the temperature of the oil when frying—if it gets too hot, it will burn, and if too cold, the exterior will be mushy.

1 (4-pound) whole chicken

1 ½ teaspoons kosher salt

¾ teaspoon black pepper

1 ½ tablespoons olive oil

2 large shallots or ½ yellow onion,
  halved

1 celery stalk, cut into 2-inch pieces

3 to 4 bacon slices, halved

SIRIOUSLY MINI

Shred the leftover meat, and use it
in quesadillas, sandwiches or pasta
dishes for the kiddos.

Susie's French Chicken

In my opinion, you never feel as accomplished in the kitchen as you do
after you've roasted your first chicken. Well, after you've successfully
roasted it, because I lit an oven mitt on fire during my initial attempt
and that didn't make me feel very accomplished. Anyhoo! Roasting a
beautiful golden bird to perfection might seem like a pro move and
therefore can scare aspiring cooks away, but if you master a simple
technique, it can actually be very simple. This recipe is case in point.
A family friend and excellent home cook, Susie, shared her method
with me years ago, and now it's the only way I roast poultry. First, it
takes about an hour, requires very few ingredients and everything
is pulled off in one heavy pot. More importantly, a small amount of
olive oil, chopped shallots and celery are all the chicken demands
to—along with its own juices—create a beautiful bubbling brown sauce
that needs nothing but a ladle to pour over the succulent meat. Those
are Susie's words...did I mention she's also a writer? Oh, and have I
acknowledged the bacon yet? There is bacon, draped over the skin,
trapping in moisture and contributing to the rich flavor of the dish.
This is the definition of "winner, winner, chicken dinner"...as long as
you don't light anything on fire.

1 Preheat the oven to 425°F.

2 Pat the chicken dry with paper towels; sprinkle evenly with the salt and
   pepper.

3 Heat the olive oil in an ovenproof Dutch oven over medium to medium-
   high. Place the chicken in the pan, breast side down, and cook until
   golden brown, about 5 minutes.

4 Turn the chicken over, and add the shallots and celery to the Dutch
   oven. Arrange the bacon slices on top of the chicken, and place in
   the oven. Bake until the bacon is crispy, about 40 minutes. Remove the
   bacon, and set it aside. Continue to bake the chicken until a meat
   thermometer inserted in the thickest portion of a thigh registers 155°F,
   15 to 20 minutes. Increase the oven temperature to a high broil without
   removing the chicken. Broil until the skin is crispy, about 5 minutes.

5 Transfer the chicken to a platter, and let rest until the internal
   temperature of the thigh registers 165°F, about 10 minutes. Chop the
   bacon, and add to the drippings mixture in the Dutch oven.

6 Slice the chicken, ladle the sauce over the chicken, and serve warm!

Quick Chicken Masala

Chicken Masala is a dish that features bite-sized pieces of tender chicken marinated in a creamy, red, curry-like sauce, usually served over rice. Interestingly, its origin is not entirely known, with both the UK and regions of India staking claims to its creation. I read Wikipedia. Nevertheless...it is a superbly flavorful dinner. While some may consider it mere take-out food, I am here to prove that making it yourself can be effortless and much more delicious. Especially with my recipe, which has the word "quick" in its title...need I say more? Oh, but I will say more, because this is my book. Simplicity is good, but what makes this dish truly shine is the wonderful warmth and depth of flavor from all the traditional Masala spices. I guess the cream doesn't hurt either, but with only a third cup for the entire dish, it's practically guilt-free. Unless you eat all of it, which is possible, but even then...balance is the answer, am I right? Just run to India the next morning, and you'll be fine.

1   Melt 2 tablespoons of the butter in a large skillet over medium-high. Add the chicken to the skillet, and cook until well browned, about 4 minutes, turning once. Remove the chicken from the skillet, and keep warm.

2   Melt the remaining tablespoon butter in the skillet. Add the onion, garlic, and ginger, and cook, stirring often, until the onion begins to soften, about 3 minutes. Add the garam masala, salt, chili powder, turmeric, cinnamon, and cayenne pepper, and cook, stirring constantly, for 30 seconds. Stir in the tomato paste, and cook, stirring constantly, for 30 seconds. Stir in the broth, scraping to loosen the browned bits from the bottom of the skillet. Add the crushed tomatoes and the chicken to the skillet, and bring to a simmer. Cover and reduce the heat to medium-low; cook until the chicken is cooked through, about 10 minutes.

3   Remove from the heat, and stir in the heavy cream. Garnish with the cilantro, and serve over the rice.

SERVES **4**
HANDS-ON TIME: **25 MINUTES**
TOTAL TIME: **25 MINUTES**

3 tablespoons unsalted butter

4 (7-ounce) boneless, skinless chicken breasts, cut into bite-sized pieces

1 small yellow onion, chopped

1 tablespoon minced garlic

1 tablespoon finely chopped fresh ginger

1 teaspoon garam masala

³/₄ teaspoon kosher salt

¹/₂ teaspoon chili powder

¹/₄ teaspoon ground turmeric

¹/₄ teaspoon ground cinnamon

¹/₄ teaspoon cayenne pepper

2 tablespoons tomato paste

³/₄ cup chicken broth

1 (14.5-ounce) can crushed tomatoes, undrained

¹/₃ cup heavy cream

¹/₂ cup fresh cilantro sprigs

Hot cooked jasmine rice

SIRIOUSLY **FANCY**

For a special extra step, heat up some store-bought naan in a skillet on the stovetop, and serve it alongside.

½ cup all-purpose flour

3 large egg whites, lightly beaten

1 cup panko (Japanese-style breadcrumbs)

1 cup grated Parmesan cheese

2 (8-ounce) boneless, skinless chicken breasts

½ teaspoon black pepper

1 teaspoon kosher salt

¼ cup olive oil

1 ½ tablespoons white wine vinegar

2 teaspoons Dijon mustard

4 cups arugula leaves (about 4 ounces)

1 small tomato, chopped

½ ripe avocado, chopped

3 tablespoons pine nuts, toasted

SIRIOUSLY IMPORTANT

Let the chicken cook undisturbed at first to encourage browning and prevent sticking.

SIRIOUSLY SIMPLE

To save time, ask the butcher at your supermarket or deli to pound the chicken for you!

Crispy Chicken Paillard

I swore I would never be a short-order cook. Nope, not me, my children would be those children that ate whatever I put in front of them without alterations or substitutions. Before I had kids, I was such a good mother! Now, in real life, with real kids, as much as I try to make one nightly meal, I've found it crucial to have a few go-to adaptable dishes. This recipe is perfect for both grown-ups and kids, which is why we make it so often. Boneless, skinless chicken breasts are pounded thinly, then lightly breaded and pan-fried to make crisp, juicy cutlets, and a refreshing, simple salad is served alongside. You can probably guess that my daughters love the chicken and skip "the green stuff" (carrots save my life), while the rest of us enjoy the arugula, tomato and avocado salad with crunchy pine nuts and a tangy Dijon dressing. It's not complex, but the presentation is refined enough to be restaurant-worthy, making it great to serve to guests (even if your guests only like chicken and carrots).

1   Place the flour in a shallow dish. Place the egg whites in a separate shallow dish. Combine the panko and ¾ cup of the Parmesan in a separate shallow dish.

2   Slice each chicken breast in half crosswise to form 2 cutlets. Place each cutlet between 2 sheets of heavy-duty plastic wrap, and pound to an even thickness (about ½ inch thick). Sprinkle the cutlets with the pepper and ¾ teaspoon of the salt. Working with 1 cutlet at a time, dredge in the flour, dip in the egg whites, and dredge in the breadcrumb mixture, shaking the excess off after each dredge.

3   Heat 1 tablespoon of the oil in a large skillet over medium-high. Add 2 chicken cutlets to the skillet and cook until golden brown and cooked through, about 3 minutes per side. Remove from the skillet. Repeat the procedure with 1 tablespoon of the oil and the remaining chicken cutlets.

4   Whisk together the vinegar, mustard, and remaining 2 tablespoons oil and ¼ teaspoon salt in a medium bowl. Add the arugula, and toss to coat. Sprinkle the arugula mixture with the tomato, avocado, pine nuts, and remaining ¼ cup Parmesan. Serve with the chicken.

Cheesy Mashed
Cauliflower
PG 185

Not-Your-Mama's Meatloaf

SERVES **6**
HANDS-ON TIME: **10 MINUTES**
TOTAL TIME: **1 HOUR
10 MINUTES**

On my culinary journey (whatever that is), I've come across many people who cringe at the thought of eating meatloaf. The retro dish has acquired somewhat of a bad reputation over the years. I accredit some of this to its name—the word "meatloaf" is certainly disturbing. Why does it have to be loaf? That's such a chunky word. It reminds me of a shoe. Who wants to eat a meat shoe? I digress. Or perhaps the meatloaf of yesteryear was bland, or dense, not like this delicious recipe in front of you. This is a moist meatloaf, light in texture but heavy in flavor and completely nourishing. It is basted during the cooking process with a savory, tangy glaze that keeps the meatloaf tender while developing a sweet crust. Nothing about this meal is bland or dense, or shoe-like. Rather, it is a yummy main entrée that would fit very nicely into your weekly dinner repertoire.

1 Preheat the oven to 350°F.

2 Combine the beef, breadcrumbs, milk, onion, egg, parsley, salt, pepper, thyme, and ½ cup of the tomato sauce.

3 Shape the mixture into a loaf, and place in a lightly greased shallow pan. Stir together the vinegar, brown sugar, mustard, Worcestershire, and remaining tomato sauce. Add the water, 1 to 2 tablespoons at a time, to thin the sauce if necessary. Pour about one-third of the tomato sauce mixture over the top of the meatloaf.

4 Bake until no longer pink in the center, about 1 hour, basting with the remaining tomato sauce mixture every 15 minutes. Sprinkle with extra parsley and serve!

1 ½ pounds ground beef chuck

1 cup fresh breadcrumbs

¼ cup whole milk

1 medium-sized yellow onion, diced

1 large egg, lightly beaten

2 tablespoons chopped fresh flat-leaf parsley, plus more for garnish

1 ½ teaspoons kosher salt

½ teaspoon black pepper

½ teaspoon fresh thyme leaves

2 (8-ounce) cans tomato sauce

3 tablespoons apple cider vinegar

3 tablespoons light brown sugar

2 tablespoons Dijon mustard

2 tablespoons Worcestershire sauce

½ cup water (optional)

SIRIOUSLY MINI

Try serving as a sandwich with mayonnaise.

SIRIOUSLY NUTRITIOUS

For a leaner dinner, swap the ground beef with ground turkey or chicken.

1 tablespoon olive oil

1 pound ground turkey

½ (1-ounce) package taco seasoning

1 (12-ounce) package frozen butternut squash puree, thawed

8 ounces uncooked pasta of your choice

2 cups chicken stock

1 (8-ounce) jar taco sauce

1 ½ cups preshredded Mexican cheese blend, plus more for garnish

¼ cup chopped scallions, white and green parts (optional)

SIRIOUSLY **NUTRITIOUS**

For an extra double-whammy of goodness, use chickpea pasta for added protein and fiber, which also makes this gluten-free!

Sneaky One-Pot Mexican Pasta

Everyone always assumes that because I write a food blog (and now a cookbook!), my kids must be fabulous eaters. EHHHHHH. That's the sound of an annoying buzzer. WRONG! I have picky, picky eaters. Right around 18 months, each of them started rejecting all healthy foods (I'm exaggerating, but you get the picture). I've felt everything from frustration, anger, shame and embarrassment over it. Yet on my good days, I realize their palates are still expanding and they won't be like this forever. Case in point: My son now eats salads! Victory! So I carry on, trying and sneaking: trying new foods, and when that doesn't work, sneaking them into their meals. Cue this cheesy, one-pot Mexican pasta with a whole lot of, wait for it, SQUASH! The frozen squash sort of melts into the ground turkey, creating a slightly sweet counterbalance to the spicier Mexican flavors. Obviously, the best part about this dish is you can make it in about 30 minutes in *one* pot. The first time I made this, my oldest and youngest gobbled it up. The stubborn middle child? Well, we had a 1950's style showdown. She sat there, crying, begging for a treat, resisting even *one* bite, and I held firm and drank a bottle of rosé by myself. Small victories, my friends.

1 Heat the olive oil in a large saucepan over medium. Add the ground turkey, and cook, stirring, until crumbled and no longer pink, about 5 minutes. Sprinkle in the taco seasoning, and cook, stirring often, until well combined, 2 to 3 minutes. Add the squash, pasta, chicken stock, and taco sauce, and bring to a boil over medium-high. Stir everything up, cover, reduce heat to low, and simmer until the pasta is al dente, 12 to 15 minutes.

2 Add the cheese, and stir until the cheese is melted and the sauce is thickened. Sprinkle with a bit more cheese and the scallions, if desired, and serve!

Asian Beef Lettuce Wraps

SERVES **4**
HANDS-ON TIME: **25 MINUTES**
TOTAL TIME: **25 MINUTES**

I am very enthusiastic about Asian cuisine. In my mid-twenties, I went to Hong Kong for a week and fell in love with the people, the culture, but mostly the food. Everything I ate fulfilled the five basic tastes: sweet, sour, bitter, salty and umami (often described as brothy or meaty). Everything, but the chicken feet...I couldn't quite wrap my head around that one (no thanks, teeny, tiny foot bones). Now, for most Asian food, I resort to restaurants or take-out; however, it's fun to experiment with the traditional flavors in your kitchen. I'm referring to flavors like sesame, ginger, soy, fish sauce and honey. I'm referring to the ingredients in this recipe! These Asian Beef Lettuce Wraps are completely satisfying as an entrée, but also work as a fun side or appetizer. They come together very easily, and if you do a little prep, you can execute everything just before company arrives. The textures are perfect, particularly the crisp lettuce that wraps it all up with a bow. Forget the take-out, or the really long flight to Asia, and make these tonight.

1   Heat the ginger, garlic, and 1 tablespoon of the oil in a large skillet over medium. Cook until the garlic begins to brown, about 2 minutes. Add the bell pepper and water chestnuts and cook until the vegetables begin to soften, 3 to 4 minutes. Remove from the skillet, and set aside.

2   Add the beef to the skillet and cook, stirring to crumble, until browned, 5 to 6 minutes. Drain, reserving 1 tablespoon of drippings in the skillet. Return the beef and bell pepper mixture to the skillet. Stir in the soy sauce, lime juice, honey, fish sauce, and remaining 1 tablespoon oil, and cook until slightly thickened and coats the beef, about 1 minute. Remove the skillet from the heat, and stir in the cilantro and mint.

3   Place about ¼ cup of the beef mixture in each lettuce leaf. Divide the cucumber evenly among the lettuce leaves. Drizzle with Sriracha, and sprinkle with peanuts before serving, if desired.

1 tablespoon finely chopped fresh ginger

2 teaspoons minced garlic

2 tablespoons toasted sesame oil

½ cup finely chopped red bell pepper

¼ cup finely chopped water chestnuts

1 pound ground beef chuck

3 tablespoons soy sauce

2 tablespoons fresh lime juice

1 ½ tablespoons honey

2 teaspoons fish sauce

¼ cup chopped fresh cilantro

2 tablespoons chopped fresh mint

12 large Bibb lettuce leaves

1 (3-inch) piece English cucumber, cut into matchsticks

Sriracha chile sauce or chile garlic sauce (optional)

Chopped roasted salted peanuts (optional)

SERVES 6
HANDS-ON TIME: 20 MINUTES
TOTAL TIME: 6 (OR 8) HOURS
20 MINUTES

Slow-Cooker Beef Bourguignon

I know exactly the first time I made Beef Bourguignon: It was August 15th, 2009. Am I a genius with an impeccable memory? Well, yes, but that's not why I remember this date. My son was born on March 15th, 2009, and Carson and I were those first time parents that literally celebrated his monthly birthday. I'm talking balloons, cake, the whole thing, although this finally fizzled out after six months or so (yes, finally). August 15th also happens to be the legendary Julia Child's birthday, and the movie about her life, *Julia & Julia*, came out around that time in 2009. After I saw it, all I wanted to do was come home and eat butter—I mean, make Beef Bourguignon—and what better occasion than my son's 5-month birthday?! Okay sure, there are probably better occasions, but it was still memorable. Over time, I've developed the recipe to incorporate a slow cooker, which increases the depth of flavor as well as making it incredibly time-friendly. This is hearty stew at its best. Serve it over buttery noodles and eat it on a cold, winter night (or a random day in August).

2 ½ pounds beef stew meat, cut into 1-inch chunks and patted dry with a paper towel

¼ cup all-purpose flour

1 teaspoon dried Italian seasoning

2 teaspoons kosher salt

1 ½ teaspoons black pepper

3 tablespoons olive oil

2 cups dry red wine (such as Pinot Noir or Cabernet Sauvignon)

2 cups beef stock

1 tablespoon tomato paste

2 cups baby potatoes

2 cups baby carrots

1 (12-ounce) package frozen pearl onions

8 ounces button mushrooms, halved

2 teaspoons chopped garlic

Hot cooked egg noodles or rice

Chopped fresh parsley

1 Combine the beef, flour, Italian seasoning, 1 teaspoon of the salt, and ¾ teaspoon of the pepper in a large bowl; stir until the beef is evenly coated.

2 Heat the olive oil in a large saucepan over medium-high. Add the beef mixture, in batches, and cook until browned, 3 to 4 minutes per side. Transfer to a 6-quart slow cooker.

3 Reduce the heat to medium; add the wine, beef stock, and tomato paste to the saucepan. Using a wooden spoon, stir, scraping up the browned bits from the bottom of the pan. Stir until the tomato paste is dissolved. Pour on top of the beef mixture in the slow cooker.

4 Stir in the potatoes, carrots, pearl onions, mushrooms, garlic, and the remaining 1 teaspoon salt and ¾ teaspoon pepper. Cover and cook until the beef and vegetables are very tender, on LOW 8 hours or HIGH 6 hours. Serve over hot cooked egg noodles or rice and sprinkle with parsley.

SIRIOUSLY SIMPLE

Have your butcher pre-cut your beef for you—they will, trust me!

SIRIOUSLY FANCY

You've probably heard this before, but cook with a good red wine—one that you would drink—as it will be a major complement to the sauce. Also, it's an excuse to pour yourself a glass while you're cooking. #necessary

Street Steak Tacos

When we lived in California, we used to celebrate Taco Tuesday every week, whether we went to a nearby restaurant or made something at home. After moving East, we still make it a priority to keep the tradition alive in our kitchen. Sometimes we make roasted chicken quesadillas, or grilled fish tostadas, but more often than not we end up with these yummy steak tacos. First, flank steak is soaked in a smoky, citrusy marinade, and then grilled until lightly charred and tender. It's served wrapped inside homemade corn tortillas, which are shockingly easy to make (with just one ingredient!). Finally—true to the simplicity of an authentic street taco—they are topped with fresh avocado pico de gallo and crumbly Cotija cheese. Your Tuesdays just got a whole lot better. After all, isn't Taco Night just an excuse to drink tequila?

1 First Make the Flank Steak: Place the steak in a large plastic freezer bag. Whisk together the next 7 ingredients. Pour the mixture into the bag; seal, and massage the marinade into the steak. Refrigerate for 1 hour or up to 24 hours.

2 Meanwhile, Start the Corn Tortillas: Combine the masa harina and salt in a large bowl; slowly pour water over. Stir until a dough forms. Gently knead into a ball, and return to the bowl. (The dough should be moist, not sticky. To test, flatten a portion into a ½-inch-thick disk. If the edges crack, add a bit more water.) Cover the bowl with a damp towel, and let stand for 30 minutes.

3 Meanwhile, Make the Avocado Pico de Gallo: Combine all the ingredients in a large bowl, and stir together. Set aside.

4 Preheat a grill to medium-high (400° to 450°F). Remove the steak from the marinade, and place on an oiled grate. Grill, uncovered, 5 to 7 minutes per side for medium-rare. Transfer to a cutting board, and let rest for 6 minutes. Cut the steak across the grain into strips.

5 Finish the Tortillas: Heat a cast-iron griddle or skillet over medium-high. Roll the dough into 2-inch balls. Working with 1 dough ball at a time, form a ½-inch-thick disk. Place the disk between 2 sheets of parchment or wax paper in a tortilla press. Press into a 6-inch round about ⅛-inch-thick (these do not need to be perfect!). Remove the paper, and place the round on the hot griddle, cooking until dry, lightly charred, and puffed, 30 seconds to 1 minute per side. Wrap in a clean kitchen towel. Repeat with the remaining dough balls to make 16.

6 Divide the steak strips evenly among the Corn Tortillas, top with the Avocado Pico de Gallo, and, if desired, crumbled Cotija cheese.

SERVES 8
HANDS-ON TIME: 20 MINUTES
TOTAL TIME: 1 HOUR
26 MINUTES

FLANK STEAK

2 pounds flank steak

½ cup olive oil

⅓ cup finely chopped fresh cilantro

1 teaspoon kosher salt

1 teaspoon black pepper

1 teaspoon ground cumin

3 garlic cloves, minced

2 tablespoons fresh lime juice

CORN TORTILLAS

2 cups masa harina

½ teaspoon kosher salt

1 ½ cups hot tap water

AVOCADO PICO DE GALLO

2 large tomatoes, finely diced

2 medium tomatillos, finely diced

½ small red onion, finely diced

1 ripe avocado, finely diced

1 jalapeño chile, finely diced (seeds and ribs optional, depending on heat preference)

⅓ cup chopped fresh cilantro

1 tablespoon fresh lime juice

1 teaspoon kosher salt

½ cup crumbled Cotija cheese, or other cheese of your choice (optional)

1 pound beef stew meat

1 teaspoon kosher salt

3/4 teaspoon black pepper

1 tablespoon canola oil

1 cup chopped carrots

3/4 cup frozen pearl onions, thawed

2 tablespoons tomato paste

1/2 cup dry red wine

1/4 cup all-purpose flour

1 tablespoon minced garlic

1 teaspoon finely chopped fresh rosemary

1 tablespoon chopped fresh thyme, plus sprigs for garnish (optional)

3 1/2 cups beef broth

1 pound Yukon Gold potatoes, cut into 1/2-inch cubes

1 (17.3-ounce) package frozen puff pastry sheets, thawed

1 large egg, lightly beaten

1 tablespoon water

Individual Beef Pot Pies

Imagine going to a dinner party and sitting down to your very own delicious Beef Pot Pie, individually served in a dainty ramekin, elegantly seasoned with thyme and black pepper...you would want to be at this dinner party, yes? And if I'm sounding too snooty with words like "dainty" and "elegant"—remember—It's Beef Pot Pie, the definition of comfort food. Besides, anything made with puff pastry is going to please just about anyone. The fact that it comes frozen but tastes heavenly will trick people into thinking you've got mad pastry skills. The real pro move in this recipe, however, is adding layers of flavor as you cook—for example, searing the beef to caramelize the meat, sautéing the vegetables in those same juices, and then deglazing the pan with tomato paste and red wine to scrape up any brown bits at the bottom. All of that contributes to the depth and richness of this dish. Every single bite is luscious, and there I go sounding snooty again. BEEF: It's what's for dinner. (There, that better?)

1 Sprinkle the beef with the salt and 1/2 teaspoon of the pepper. Heat the oil in a Dutch oven over medium-high. Add the beef to the Dutch oven, and cook, stirring occasionally, until browned on all sides, about 8 minutes. Remove the beef from the Dutch oven.

2 Add the carrots and onions to the Dutch oven, and cook, stirring occasionally, until slightly softened, about 6 minutes. Add the tomato paste, and cook, stirring often, about 1 minute. Pour in the wine, and cook until the liquid is nearly evaporated, 1 to 2 minutes, stirring and scraping to loosen any browned bits from the bottom of the Dutch oven. Add the flour, garlic, rosemary, and 2 teaspoons of the thyme, and cook, stirring often, 1 to 2 minutes. Pour in the broth, and bring to a boil. Return the beef to the Dutch oven, cover and reduce the heat to medium-low. Cook until the beef is almost tender, about 45 minutes. Add the potatoes and cook, uncovered, until the beef and potatoes are tender, about 15 minutes.

3 Preheat the oven to 400°F. Cut the puff pastry sheets into 6 (6-inch) squares. Divide the beef mixture among 6 (8-ounce) ramekins; top each with 1 puff pastry square.

4 Combine the egg and 1 tablespoon water in a small dish. Brush the puff pastry with the egg mixture, and sprinkle with the remaining 1 teaspoon thyme and remaining 1/4 teaspoon pepper. Bake until golden brown, 20 to 25 minutes. Sprinkle with extra thyme sprigs, if desired, and serve!

Greek Lamb Burgers with Tzatziki

SERVES **4**
HANDS-ON TIME: **15 MINUTES**
TOTAL TIME: **20 MINUTES**

My entire family adores lollipop lamb chops. The kids have all spent countless dinners gnawing the meat off the bone, even as little (chubby) babies. However, because we usually reserve that sort of meal for fancier occasions, on more average nights, we rely on these delicious Greek burgers to satisfy our lamb craving. There is so much to love about this recipe. These burgers are more unique than plain old beef patties and packed with savory flavors. They take almost no time to make. They are served with a creamy, homemade tzatiki sauce, which, once you make one time, you will want to make over and over again. They can be grilled in or outdoors, making it an ideal year-round meal. In short, these are delicious, juicy burgers. Serve them on soft buns with fresh spinach, salty feta cheese, sliced tomatoes and the cucumber-yogurt sauce dreams are made of, and you'll have a perfect dinner for guests, for yourself or for your lamb-loving babies.

1 pound ground lamb

3 tablespoons grated red onion

3 tablespoons finely chopped fresh flat-leaf parsley

1 tablespoon balsamic vinegar

2 teaspoons minced garlic

1 teaspoon kosher salt

1 teaspoon black pepper

½ unpeeled English cucumber

½ cup plain whole-milk Greek yogurt

1 tablespoon chopped fresh dill

1 tablespoon fresh lemon juice

1 cup baby spinach leaves

4 soft potato hamburger buns

4 tomato slices

½ cup crumbled feta cheese

1   Combine the lamb, onion, parsley, vinegar, 1 teaspoon of the garlic, and ¾ teaspoon each of the salt and pepper in a medium bowl; stir gently until just combined. Divide the mixture into 4 portions. Shape each into a patty.

2   Heat a lightly greased grill pan over medium-high. Add the patties to the pan, and cook until a thermometer inserted in thickest portion registers 140°F for medium, 4 to 5 minutes per side, or until desired degree of doneness. Let stand 5 to 10 minutes.

3   Meanwhile, grate the cucumber to measure 1 cup. Place on a clean towel, wrap the towel around the cucumber, and twist tightly to remove as much liquid as possible. Combine the grated cucumber, yogurt, dill, lemon juice, and remaining 1 teaspoon garlic and ¼ teaspoon each salt and pepper in a small bowl.

4   Divide the spinach among the bottom halves of the buns; top each with 1 patty, one-fourth of the cucumber sauce, 1 tomato slice, and about 2 tablespoons feta. Cover with the tops of the buns, and serve immediately.

Carnivores.

SIRIOUSLY **VARIED**

Not in the mood for lamb? You can easily swap it out with ground turkey, chicken or beef.

SIRIOUSLY **SIMPLE**

Make the sauce ahead of time, or even better, make extra so you have leftovers for dolloping on just about anything!

1 teaspoon minced garlic

3 tablespoons unsalted butter

1 cup panko (Japanese-style breadcrumbs)

½ teaspoon ground cumin

1 (1-pound) pork tenderloin, trimmed

½ teaspoon light brown sugar

½ teaspoon black pepper

1 teaspoon kosher salt

2 Fuji apples, chopped

2 shallots, sliced

1 cup spiced apple cider

3 teaspoons apple cider vinegar

Hot cooked rice

Sour cream (optional)

Fresh thyme sprigs (optional)

Pork Tenderloin with Sautéed Apples

This dish tastes like football games on Friday nights, like picnics and fireworks, like country music and bald eagles and watery beer and Oprah. What is this nonsense I'm spewing at you? I'm trying to articulate that pork paired with apples tastes classic; like something truly American (which might not be accurate but I'm no historian). A dinner of pork chops and applesauce feels very retro—maybe because Peter Brady turned it into a catchphrase on *The Brady Bunch*—and that vintage combination is what inspired me to give the time-honored meal a modern twist. Instead of chops, I love to cook with pork tenderloin, which is a leaner cut and can be prepared much quicker. Instead of applesauce, I love to slowly sauté apples with shallots, cider and vinegar until they soften and caramelize. A smoky, panko crust is rubbed on the meat and creates a crispy exterior while locking in moisture. This tender pork will almost melt in your mouth, and combined with the sweet, spiced, buttery apples, turns a blast-from-the-past dinner into a grand slam on an autumn day. #America

1   Preheat the oven to 400°F. Place the garlic and 1 tablespoon of the butter in a large nonstick skillet over medium-high. Cook until the garlic starts to brown, 2 to 3 minutes. Add the panko and cumin, and cook, stirring often, until the panko is golden brown, 3 to 4 minutes. Transfer to a shallow dish, and let cool for about 5 minutes.

2   Sprinkle the pork with the brown sugar, pepper, and ½ teaspoon of the salt. Roll the pork in the panko mixture, pressing to adhere. Place on a rack over a rimmed baking sheet, and bake until a thermometer inserted in the thickest portion registers 145°F, about 25 minutes. Remove from the oven, and let rest for about 10 minutes before slicing.

3   Meanwhile, heat 1 tablespoon of the butter in a large nonstick skillet over medium-high. Add the apples and shallots, and cook, stirring occasionally, until the apples start to brown and soften, about 15 minutes. Add the cider, vinegar, and remaining 1 tablespoon butter and ½ teaspoon salt to the skillet; cook until the apples are tender-crisp and the sauce is creamy, about 2 minutes. Serve the pork and apples over the rice; dollop with sour cream and sprinkle with fresh thyme, if desired.

-Roasted
els Sprouts
G 193

Slow-Cooked Pulled Pork Chalupas

SERVES 10
HANDS-ON TIME: 55 MINUTES
TOTAL TIME: 7 HOURS
10 MINUTES

At nearly every large family gathering growing up, my mom would make Pork Chalupas. She started by soaking beans overnight (which legit made the house smell like farts), and the next day she would begin a timely process of boiling meat, simmering and marinating for what seemed like hours. (The aromas improved exponentially at this point.) The shredded pork was then piled on top of chips with a plethora of toppings to choose from, making the meal a huge hit amongst everyone. Since that time, I've developed my own method of cooking this flavorful feast, and that is using a Crock-Pot. Chester! (See: Slow-Cooker Mac & Cheese for "Chester" explanation.) In this recipe, the slow cooker does all the hard work for you and what you're left with is super-tender, savory meat. Instead of the chips my mom used, I like to lightly fry tortillas until they puff up and crisp—trust me, that small effort raises the bar from excellent to extraordinary. Once topped with velvety refried beans (#nosmell), shredded pork, salty queso, creamy avocado, tangy pico and bright cilantro, you're left with a dinner you will want to make again and again.

1 Combine the salt, chili powder, cumin, cinnamon, and pepper in a small bowl. Rub the spice mixture over the pork.

2 Place the onion and garlic in the bottom of a 6- to 8-quart slow cooker. Add the beer and broth. Place the pork on top, cover, and cook on HIGH until the pork is very tender, about 6 hours, or on LOW for 8 hours. Remove the pork from the cooker, and let stand for about 15 minutes. Coarsely shred the pork, and return it to the cooker; toss gently to coat with the cooking liquid.

3 Heat the refried beans in a small pan over medium-low, according to the can directions; cover and keep warm.

4 Heat the oil in a medium skillet over medium-high until shimmering. Add 1 tortilla and cook until lightly puffed, 2 to 3 minutes per side. Transfer the tortilla to a paper-lined tray, and repeat with the remaining tortillas.

5 Divide the beans, pork mixture, avocado, queso fresco, Avocado Pico de Gallo, and cilantro evenly among the tortillas, and serve immediately with lime wedges, if desired.

1 ½ tablespoons kosher salt

1 tablespoon chili powder

2 teaspoons ground cumin

1 ½ teaspoons ground cinnamon

1 teaspoon black pepper

1 (4- to 5-pound) boneless pork shoulder

1 large white onion, sliced

3 garlic cloves, sliced

1 cup Mexican beer

½ cup chicken broth

1 (16-ounce) can refried beans

½ cup canola oil

20 (6-inch) flour tortillas

Ripe avocados, cut into wedges

¾ cup crumbled queso fresco (fresh Mexican cheese)

¾ cup Avocado Pico de Gallo (see page 155)

⅓ cup chopped fresh cilantro

Lime wedges (optional)

SIRIOUSLY SIMPLE

You could fry the tortillas in 2 pans to cut down the time: same process, just use 2 pans and cook simultaneously.

SERVES **6**
HANDS-ON TIME: **30 MINUTES**
TOTAL TIME: **30 MINUTES**

2 teaspoons canola oil

12 ounces sweet Italian pork sausage, casings removed

1 ½ cups chopped white onion

½ cup diced celery

2 teaspoons minced garlic

2 teaspoons chili powder

2 teaspoons ground cumin

1 teaspoon kosher salt

¾ teaspoon black pepper

1 tablespoon all-purpose flour

3 cups chicken stock

2 (4-ounce) cans diced green chiles, undrained

2 cups blue corn tortilla chips

6 tablespoons sour cream

1 jalapeño chile, sliced

1 large ripe avocado, diced

¼ cup fresh cilantro leaves

SIRIOUSLY **SIMPLE**

To remove the casings from Italian sausage, pinch one end of the link, and slide your fingers down the link, forcing the sausage out.

Mexican Pork Soup

I love sweet Italian pork sausage. The flavors are bold, the meat is fatty and rich, it is able to caramelize and crisp up beautifully but also remains juicy and succulent...what's not to love? My favorite thing to make with Italian pork sausage is Mexican Pork Soup. Say whaaaat? Yeah, I'm wild like that. The subtle sweetness that the pork offers complements all the strong, spicy flavors from the soup in a delightful way. What's even more appealing is how quickly you can whip this up, especially if you prep your ingredients beforehand (which I always do because I like to pretend I'm constantly being filmed for a nonexistent cooking show). It's got heat, but if you skip the jalapeños it's not too spicy, and I should know because my picky toddler drinks the broth like a boss. This makes an excellent weeknight dinner (and even better lunch leftovers), but would also be perfect to serve a hungry weekend crowd.

1   Heat the oil in a large saucepan over medium-high. Add the sausage, and cook, stirring to crumble, until browned, 4 to 5 minutes. Add the onion and celery, and cook, stirring occasionally, until tender and lightly browned, 4 to 5 minutes. Add the garlic, chili powder, cumin, salt, and black pepper, and cook, stirring constantly, 30 seconds. Stir in the flour, and cook, stirring constantly, 1 minute. Stir in the broth and green chiles. Finely crush half of the tortilla chips, and stir into the soup. (Coarsely crush the remaining chips, and set aside.) Bring the soup to a boil; cover and reduce the heat to medium-low. Simmer until the flavors are incorporated, about 15 minutes.

2   Divide the soup evenly among 6 bowls; top evenly with the sour cream, jalapeño, avocado, and cilantro. Sprinkle with the reserved crushed chips.

Tuna Casserole with Orecchiette

SERVES 6
HANDS-ON TIME: **10 MINUTES**
TOTAL TIME: **25 MINUTES**

Tuna Casserola, as we referred to it growing up, was one of my favorite weeknight dinners. I'm not sure why we called it that; most likely it was some cute mispronunciation—like how my youngest daughter wants to make sure her blankets are "flap" at night (read: flat). I can still taste my mom's version of the classic dish, which consisted of pasta shells, cream of mushroom soup, black olives and, of course, tuna. Oh, and I mustn't leave out the crushed potato chips on top (best, part). There is nothing wrong with that version—that version represents my youth—however once I started cooking my own dinners, I decided to give the familiar flavors a modern twist. Just like the old-fashioned rendition, this is creamy, cheesy and finished with a nice crunch thanks to some homemade fried leeks. It is comfort food without any cook-all-day-long effort. My mother approves, but still calls it "casserola"—and when my daughter is in her forties, I will still probably ask if she wants her blankets "flap."

1 pound uncooked orecchiette pasta (or shells or spirals)

2 tablespoons olive oil

1 small yellow onion, finely diced

4 ounces button mushrooms, finely diced

3 tablespoons all-purpose flour

1 cup chicken stock

1 cup whole milk

1 1/2 cups grated white Cheddar cheese

1 1/2 teaspoons kosher salt

1/2 teaspoon freshly ground black pepper

1 (12-ounce) can solid white tuna in spring water, drained and flaked

1 cup frozen sweet peas

1 medium leek

Vegetable oil

1 Preheat the oven to 425°F.

2 Cook the pasta in a large saucepan according to the package instructions until al dente. Drain and set aside.

3 Heat the olive oil in a saucepan over medium. Add the onion and mushrooms, and sauté until they begin to caramelize, about 5 minutes Stir in the flour, and sauté for 1 minute.

4 Whisk in the chicken stock until blended. Whisk in the milk and 1 cup of the Cheddar cheese. Bring to a boil over medium-high, whisking constantly. Reduce the heat to low, and simmer, whisking constantly, until the sauce begins to thicken, 5 to 7 minutes. Whisk in the salt and pepper.

5 Remove from the heat, and stir in the tuna, peas, and pasta. Spoon into a lightly greased 13- x 9-inch baking dish, and sprinkle the top with the remaining 1/2 cup Cheddar cheese. Bake, uncovered, until the top is bubbly and golden, 15 to 20 minutes.

6 Meanwhile, very thinly slice the white and pale green parts of the leek. Rinse under water in a colander.

7 Heat about 1 inch of vegetable oil in a small pot over medium. Add the sliced leek, and cook, stirring often, until golden and crispy, about 10 minutes. Using a slotted spoon, remove the leek to drain on paper towels. Sprinkle the crispy leeks on top of the casserole before serving.

Miso Shrimp Stir-Fry with Eggs and Crispy Rice

2 tablespoons soy sauce

1 tablespoon unseasoned rice vinegar

1 tablespoon white miso paste

¼ cup toasted sesame oil

1 pound raw peeled and deveined large shrimp

¼ teaspoon kosher salt

¼ teaspoon black pepper

4 large eggs

1 tablespoon whole milk

1 cup diagonally sliced sugar snap peas

1 cup chopped yellow bell pepper

1 small red onion, cut into wedges

2 teaspoons minced garlic

2 teaspoons finely chopped fresh ginger

2 cups cooked white long-grain rice, chilled

¼ cup chopped fresh cilantro

SIRIOUSLY **SPICY**

For some extra date-night spice, sprinkle red pepper flakes on top.

The first time I tried miso was at a fancy sushi restaurant with Carson. We weren't dating at that point, but we were "crushing"—is that a thing? I'm too old and married now. Dating terms go over my head, like "ghosting" to me is when kids drop candy on your doorstep, ring the bell, and run. Anyway, at this sushi restaurant, I definitely had a crush on him and he was definitely trying to impress me with spicy tuna and lychee martinis. The miso cod, however, was something else entirely. That sweet, salty, almost earthy flavor resulted in love at first bite, and I knew I would marry it—I mean, Carson. I'm talking about him, not food. *Yeah.* It's many years later now, but I still love miso, especially since I've discovered how easy it is to cook with it. Combining shrimp with miso is one of my favorite pairings, and serving it with tender, stir-fried veggies, lightly scrambled eggs and crispy rice makes a beyond tasty dinner. Yup, the rice here is quickly fried in sesame oil, and it's ridiculous. Food is capable of triggering memories, and with the flavors of this meal I'm always reminded of that flirtatious dinner years ago. (Even though we eat it in sweatpants now watching TV.)

1   Preheat the oven to 400°F. Combine the soy sauce, vinegar, miso paste, and 2 tablespoons of the sesame oil in a small bowl, stirring with a whisk until the miso paste dissolves; set aside.

2   Place the shrimp in an even layer on a baking sheet. Sprinkle with the salt and black pepper. Bake until they turn pink, about 5 minutes.

3   Combine the eggs and milk in a small bowl, stirring with a whisk. Heat 1 tablespoon of the sesame oil in a wok or large nonstick skillet over high. Add the egg mixture, and cook, stirring occasionally to produce large curds, until almost done, about 1 minute. Remove the eggs from the wok, and chop into ¼-inch pieces.

4   Add the peas, bell pepper, and onion to the wok, and cook, stirring often, until slightly charred, about 3 minutes. Add the garlic and ginger, and cook, stirring often, about 1 minute. Add the soy sauce mixture, bring to a boil, and cook about 1 minute. Transfer to a bowl.

5   Heat the remaining 1 tablespoon sesame oil in the wok. Add the rice, and cook on high, stirring often, until just brown and crispy, 4 to 6 minutes. Add the shrimp, egg, and vegetable mixture, and stir to combine. Sprinkle with the cilantro, and serve immediately.

Spaghetti Squash
Aglio e Olio
PG 198

Chilean Sea Bass with Tomato–White Wine Sauce

SERVES **4**
HANDS-ON TIME: **10 MINUTES**
TOTAL TIME: **25 MINUTES**

During my twenties, a few friends and I started a Gourmet Dinner Club. I think we successfully got together to cook once, but the intention was there. (Actually, the real intention was to woo Carson with home-cooked meals...shhh, don't tell him that.) For that singular, memorable dinner, we made a Chilean Sea Bass with lots of garlic and wine (which we drank most of). I'll never forget how dignified I felt that night, even though at the time I shared a full-sized Ikea bed with my roommate (#truth). Anyway, Chilean Sea Bass is more costly than other flaky, white fishes, so it seemed appropriate for our elite and fancy* club (*not really either of those things). Sea bass has a delicate, buttery, always-tender center, making it worthy of any dinner—extravagant or not. Over the years, I continue to try out new ways to prepare this elegant fish, and baking it nestled in a savory tomato–white wine sauce is one of my favorite methods. The flavors are deep, and the textures varied. My neighbor actually taught me this technique, so I guess all that's left to do is form a snobby, culinary society with her. Be right back.

½ cup panko (Japanese-style breadcrumbs)

2 teaspoons minced garlic

1 teaspoon finely chopped fresh rosemary

¼ cup olive oil

½ cup diced tomato

½ cup dry white wine

1 tablespoon sliced garlic

1¼ teaspoons kosher salt

4 (6-ounce) Chilean sea bass fillets

½ teaspoon black pepper

Lemon wedges (optional)

1   Preheat the oven to 425°F. Heat a medium skillet over medium-high. Add the panko, minced garlic, and rosemary, and cook, stirring occasionally, until the panko is lightly toasted, about 3 minutes. Remove from the heat, and drizzle with 2 tablespoons of the oil, stirring until the crumbs are well coated.

2   Combine the tomato, wine, sliced garlic, ¼ teaspoon of the salt, and the remaining 2 tablespoons oil in a 13- x 9-inch baking dish. Pat the fish dry with paper towels, and sprinkle with the pepper and the remaining 1 teaspoon salt. Nestle the fish into the tomato mixture in the baking dish, and top evenly with the panko mixture. Bake until a thermometer inserted in the thickest portion registers 140°F, 14 to 16 minutes. Serve the fish with the sauce and, if desired, lemon wedges.

Carson's Grilled Swordfish with Crispy Capers

3 tablespoons fresh lemon juice

2 garlic cloves, minced

2 teaspoons finely chopped fresh oregano

1 teaspoon kosher salt

½ teaspoon black pepper

½ cup plus 2 tablespoons extra-virgin olive oil

4 (5-ounce) swordfish steaks

1 (3.5-ounce) bottle capers, drained

Fresh basil leaves

Lemon wedges

SIRIOUSLY **IMPORTANT**

Reheating most any fish will dry it out, so either eat this immediately or eat the leftovers cold in a sandwich or salad.

During the summers, we spend a lot of time in the San Clemente area of California. It feels like home away from home, and over the years, we've established ourselves as "regulars" at many of the local joints. We know just where to go for the best shaved ice, the best sushi with a view, the best dirt-cheap burrito and the best dive-bar cocktail. You can probably imagine that we are SUPER regular at that last place. Anyway, we've also discovered great seafood markets where we love to buy salmon, halibut and swordfish, and when we do, my husband takes over. Carson has perfected numerous seafood dishes, but one of my favorites is his Grilled Swordfish. It's a robust, meaty fish that if cooked properly can still be tender and juicy, and because of its firm flesh, he's found grilling is the way to achieve that goal. He assembles a simple marinade of lemon juice, garlic, oregano and olive oil, cooks the fish for just a few minutes per side, and drizzles the remaining sauce over the top. I added the crispy capers, however, because I'm a control freak and can't let him have all the glory. Besides, that salty crunch is a perfect complement to the moist fish (sort of how he and I are to each other #romance). This dish tastes like our West Coast "home," and I hope it reminds you of a relaxed, summer day.

1   Whisk together the lemon juice, garlic, oregano, salt, pepper, and ½ cup of the olive oil in a small bowl. Reserve ¼ cup of the lemon-oil mixture, and set aside. Brush the remaining lemon-oil mixture over both sides of the swordfish steaks, and let sit while you make the capers.

2   Heat the remaining 2 tablespoons olive oil in a small skillet over medium-high. Add the capers, and sauté for 2 to 3 minutes. Remove from the heat, and drain on paper towels.

3   Preheat a grill to medium-high (400° to 450°F) or heat a grill pan over medium-high. Grill or cook the swordfish until firm and a thermometer in the thickest portion registers 145°F, about 3 minutes per side, depending on the thickness of the fish. Top with the crispy capers and fresh basil, drizzle with the reserved lemon-oil mixture, and serve immediately with lemon wedges on the side.

Sautéed Spinach
with Browned
Butter
PG 199

FIVE

Sidekicks

Batman and Robin, Wayne and Garth, Lucy and
Ethel...these are all examples of leading figures with
their buddy sidekicks. Every primary force needs good
backup, am I right, ladies? Isn't that what the male
species is meant for anyway? (Tee hee hee.) This is also
the case when it comes to food. For every main entrée,
there is a delicious side dish that perfectly accompanies
it. Think about it. Can you imagine eating steak without
potatoes, or hamburgers without French fries, or tacos
without rice and beans? They go hand-in-hand, like a
marriage of sorts. A food fusion...a culinary coupling...a
merger of meals...I'll stop this now.

What I'm trying to say is, a good side dish is meant to accomplish so much. First, it should complement your meal with flavor and texture. Consider how the savory loves the sweet, the smooth and creamy yearns for a crunch, or how something hot and spicy craves a cooling down factor. Second, your side should satisfy a group of food that your main dish is not fulfilling. For example, you don't want to eat meat with a side of meat...unless you're a carnivore caveman (and I'm not judging if you are). Finally, and this goes hand in hand with my second point, your plate should look pretty. That might sound silly, but as they always say, you should "eat the rainbow" and "they" are very smart. If your meal is all one color, then you're most likely not eating a variety of foods. All of these things contribute to a complete feast that will keep your belly content.

However, while harmony is all fine and well, the best part about the side dishes in this chapter is how good they are individually. Each recipe is simple, yet delightfully tasty and would make a delicious meal unto itself. The Roasted Carrot and Pumpkin Seed Salad would be a delicious lunch, the Buffalo-Baked Cauliflower makes a perfect game-day appetizer, and the Zucchini Linguini with Pistachio-and-Pea Pesto is a gratifying vegetarian dinner. Or, for a fun twist at any food-centered gathering, simply make a bunch of these sides to pass around and skip the main entirely. After all, the best part of Thanksgiving isn't the turkey, but everything that comes with it.

In conclusion...actually I don't have a conclusion; this isn't a term paper. Side dishes are great, and that is all. They are like cheerleaders, rooting on the main attraction, yet equally important to the big picture. They will help you achieve an appetizing evenness, and like they always say, balance is the key to life.

SERVES **4**

HANDS-ON TIME: **20 MINUTES**

TOTAL TIME: **50 MINUTES**

1/3 cup raw pumpkin seeds

5 tablespoons plus 1 teaspoon olive oil

1 1/2 teaspoons kosher salt

6 large carrots, peeled and diagonally sliced

3/4 teaspoon black pepper

1 1/2 tablespoons fresh lime juice

1 teaspoon ground cumin

1 teaspoon honey

1 large ripe avocado, chopped

3 cups baby arugula

1/3 cup crumbled queso fresco (fresh Mexican cheese)

SIRIOUSLY SPICY

I first made a salad similar to this on a weekend girl's trip. We added jalapeños, and my friend who was chopping them touched the seeds, and then itched her nose (which is a polite way of saying she picked her nose). I'm sure you can imagine what ensued...tears of laughter, shrieks of pain, and my friend snorting milk out of a shot glass. While it is a (fond?) memory, I have removed the jalapeños from this salad, but you can certainly add them back if you're not afraid of heat (or washing your hands while you cook).

Roasted Carrot and Pumpkin Seed Salad

Did you know that salads don't always have to be a combination of cold vegetables and dressing? Nope, warm salads are the bomb, if you're okay with me using the term "bomb" (and you shouldn't be). I am a huge fan of roasting vegetables and combining them with a dark, leafy green. The starring duo of this salad is the appetizing combination of creamy avocados and sweet, roasted carrots. Not only do the flavors complement one another, they are also a textural pair met in heaven. Pair carrots and avocado together on a bed of peppery arugula with crunchy pumpkin seeds and salty queso fresco. To round out the dish, make a simple vinaigrette from smoky cumin and fresh lime juice. This is a great side for roasted chicken or a simple grilled fish.

1. Preheat the oven to 400°F. Toss together the pumpkin seeds, 1 teaspoon of the oil, and 1/4 teaspoon of the salt on a rimmed baking sheet. Bake until lightly toasted, 6 to 8 minutes, stirring once halfway through baking.

2. Toss together the carrots, 2 tablespoons of the olive oil, 1 teaspoon of the salt, and 1/2 teaspoon of the pepper on a rimmed baking sheet. Bake until tender, 15 to 20 minutes. Cool in the pan on a wire rack for 10 minutes.

3. Whisk together the lime juice, cumin, honey, and remaining 3 tablespoons oil and 1/4 teaspoon each of salt and pepper in a small bowl.

4. Gently toss together the carrots, pumpkin seeds, avocado, and vinaigrette in a large bowl. Place the arugula on a serving platter; arrange the carrot mixture on top. Sprinkle with the queso fresco.

Rainbow Potato Salad with Crispy Shallots

SERVES **8**
HANDS-ON TIME: **30 MINUTES**
TOTAL TIME: **55 MINUTES**

I basically win every barbeque by bringing this potato salad. I know that backyard hangs aren't necessarily competitions, and therefore you can't really "win" a barbeque, but...let's be honest, I do. And if this becomes your go-to side dish, you will win, too! It is a huge hit, every time. Some potato salads are overly tossed in thick dressing, but in this dish each tender bite of potato is perfectly coated with a delicious combination of mayonnaise, buttermilk and whole-grain mustard. However, the real reason this salad wins at life (I've moved on from winning barbeques) is that it's topped with crispy fried shallots. The crunchy texture complements the tender potatoes perfectly. In fact, I won't be mad at you if you make too many and save the rest for snacking purposes. Winning!

2 pounds multicolored baby potatoes, halved

1/2 cup mayonnaise

1/4 cup chopped celery

2 tablespoons whole buttermilk

2 tablespoons whole-grain mustard

2 tablespoons chopped fresh chives

1 tablespoon white vinegar

1 1/2 teaspoons kosher salt

3/4 teaspoon black pepper

1/4 teaspoon paprika

2 large hard-cooked eggs, peeled and chopped

2 shallots, thinly sliced crosswise

1/3 cup all-purpose flour

1/3 cup canola oil

1 Bring a large stockpot of salted water to a boil over high. Add the potatoes, and cook until fork-tender, about 12 minutes. Drain, and cool for 15 minutes.

2 Stir together the mayonnaise, celery, buttermilk, mustard, chives, vinegar, salt, pepper, and paprika in a large bowl. Stir in the potatoes and chopped eggs, lightly smashing to break apart the potatoes.

3 Toss the shallots in flour, shaking off any excess. Heat the oil in a large skillet over medium-high. Fry the shallots until golden brown and crispy, 3 to 4 minutes. Drain on paper towels. Serve the shallots sprinkled over the potato salad.

1 (1 ½-pound) rutabaga, peeled
   and cut into ¼-inch sticks

2 tablespoons olive oil

1 tablespoon chopped fresh
   rosemary

½ teaspoon black pepper

1 ¼ teaspoons sea salt

Rosemary-Rutabaga Fries

If you have kids, you've probably consumed one too many French fries as a parent. My personal favorite is when I think I'm being healthy ordering a salad at a restaurant only to finish off their entire plate of fries. As a lover of the food group (fries are a food group, right?), I also love coming up with healthier alternatives. Rutabagas are root vegetables that are not only fun to pronounce, they are an excellent source of vitamins, potassium and fiber...all nutrients my children often miss in their fried food diet. Have I mentioned the delicious flavor? While slightly bitter in its raw form, once cooked a rutabaga is richly sweet and savory at the same time. Here, they are cut into sticks, tossed with olive oil and simply roasted with fresh rosemary, sea salt and pepper. You will not feel guilty for devouring an entire plate of these.

1 Preheat the oven to 425°F. Place the rutabaga sticks in a large bowl; drizzle with the olive oil, and sprinkle with the rosemary, pepper, and 1 teaspoon of the salt. Use your hands to toss, making sure to coat well.

2 Place the rutabaga fries in an even layer on a baking sheet, and bake for 15 to 20 minutes, shaking the pan a few times to ensure even cooking. Remove the fries from the oven; sprinkle with the remaining ¼ teaspoon salt. Serve hot.

2 pounds sweet potatoes, peeled

3 tablespoons olive oil

1 ¼ teaspoons kosher salt

¾ teaspoon chili powder

½ teaspoon paprika, plus more for garnish

½ teaspoon black pepper

¼ teaspoon cayenne pepper

¼ teaspoon garlic powder

Flaky sea salt, for garnish

Spicy Sweet Potato Rounds

Photograph on page 138

I distinctly remember the time of my life when I stopped ordering take-out every night. I lived with some friends who shared my realization that it was more fun—not to mention financially responsible—to cook for ourselves. Sure, we almost always stuck to some form of chicken as our entrée, but we experimented more with our sides, and these Spicy Sweet Potato Rounds were born out of those endeavors. This dish is not only cheap and easy to make, it is addictively sweet and savory with a zing of spice. It helps to pick out sweet potatoes with uniform shapes, which means everything cooks more evenly. Also, make sure to not crowd the pans so that the potatoes don't over-steam. Now put down those take-out menus and get ready to devour this yummy side dish.

1 Preheat the oven to 450°F with the oven rack in the upper third of the oven.

2 Cut the potatoes into ½-inch-thick rounds. Spread in a single layer on 2 rimmed baking sheets. Drizzle with the oil to coat. Sprinkle with the salt, chili powder, paprika, black pepper, cayenne pepper, and garlic powder.

3 Bake until tender and slightly charred, 25 to 30 minutes. Transfer the potatoes to a serving platter, and garnish with extra paprika and flaky sea salt.

Cheesy Mashed Cauliflower

Photograph on page 146

SERVES **4**

HANDS-ON TIME: **10 MINUTES**
TOTAL TIME: **25 MINUTES**

We started making mashed cauliflower shortly after our first child was born, and also after realizing that all we were doing was sitting at home, coddling our son, and eating our faces off. Needless to say, we needed to reel it in a bit. Turning cauliflower into a mashed potato-type dish is a deceivingly yummy way to create healthier sides that still taste comforting. It requires very few, easy-to-find ingredients and yet the dish feels fancy enough to serve at your Thanksgiving table. It is creamy, it is heavenly, and, if you have a little one at home, it makes great baby food!

2 heads cauliflower, cut into florets

²/₃ cup shredded white Cheddar cheese

¼ cup heavy cream or whole milk

1 teaspoon sea salt

¼ teaspoon black pepper

1   Fill a large saucepan with 1 inch or so of water, and bring to a boil over high. Add the cauliflower florets, and cover, venting the lid slightly to let out steam. Reduce the heat to medium, and cook until the cauliflower is easily pierced with a fork, 15 to 20 minutes.

2   Drain and place the cauliflower back in the pan over medium heat. Cook, stirring constantly, until the excess moisture is released, about 3 minutes.

3   Place the cauliflower in a blender, and process until smooth, about 5 seconds. Spoon the cauliflower puree back into the pan over medium.

4   Stir in the cheese and cream until the cheese has melted. Sprinkle with the salt and pepper, and serve.

SIRIOUSLY **SIMPLE**

If you don't want to use a blender, you can use a potato masher for a chunkier version of this dish. Alternatively, an immersion blender will provide a creamier mash and is easier to clean than a traditional blender.

Flashback to when one kid seemed challenging.

Cauliflower
Steaks with
Gremolata
PG 189

Buffalo-Baked
Cauliflower
PG 188

SERVES **4**
HANDS-ON TIME: **15 MINUTES**
TOTAL TIME: **1 HOUR**

½ cup all-purpose flour

2 ¼ teaspoons kosher salt

1 ¼ teaspoons black pepper

1 cup panko (Japanese-style breadcrumbs)

2 large egg whites, well beaten

16 ounces cauliflower florets (from 1 medium head cauliflower)

⅓ cup buffalo-style sauce (such as Frank's RedHot)

¼ cup plain whole-milk Greek yogurt

¼ cup crumbled blue cheese

3 tablespoons whole buttermilk

3 tablespoons mayonnaise

1 teaspoon fresh lemon juice

SIRIOUSLY MINI

As mentioned above, my kids love cauliflower but aren't into spicy things so when I'm making it for them, I skip the buffalo sauce step.

Buffalo-Baked Cauliflower

Photograph on page 187

Okay, so I'm sort of obsessed with cauliflower. Do you say caul-EE-flower or caul-IH-flower? Never mind, no matter. All that matters is that everyone in my house loves the vegetable, so it's a keeper! Do you know what else is a keeper? Buffalo sauce. Buffalo ANYTHING. The popular hot sauce is most associated with fried chicken wings, but that's not exactly the healthiest way to enjoy the sensation. Enter: Buffalo-Baked Cauliflower. The cauliflower is coated in an egg white/panko mixture, which keeps it light and nutritious while still tasting hearty. Then, it is dipped in a Greek yogurt–based dipping sauce (okay, with a teeeeny bit of mayo) that almost tastes sinful. It is a perfect side for buffalo-lovers, and would even make a great appetizer for a game-day gathering.

1   Preheat the oven to 425°F with the oven rack 8 inches from the heat. Combine the flour, 1 teaspoon of the salt, and ½ teaspoon of the pepper in a shallow bowl. Combine the panko, 1 teaspoon of the salt, and ½ teaspoon of the pepper in a second shallow bowl. Place the egg whites in a third shallow bowl. Working in batches, dredge the cauliflower in flour mixture, shaking off the excess. Coat the cauliflower in egg whites, and dredge in the panko, shaking off the excess. Place on a lightly greased, aluminum foil-lined rimmed baking sheet. Bake until the cauliflower is tender and golden, 35 to 45 minutes. Remove the cauliflower from the oven, and increase the temperature to a high broil.

2   Toss together the roasted cauliflower and buffalo sauce in a large bowl. Spread the coated cauliflower in a single layer on the baking sheet, and broil until lightly charred, about 4 minutes.

3   Stir together the yogurt, blue cheese, buttermilk, mayonnaise, lemon juice, and remaining ¼ teaspoon each salt and pepper. Serve with the cauliflower.

Cauliflower Steaks
with Gremolata

Photograph on page 186

Give me a C! Give me an A! Give me a...forget it, cauliflower is too long of a word to spell out in cheer form. I'm just too excited to share another recipe with you based on the white, fluffy vegetable! While chopping up a head of cauliflower into florets is all fine and good, slicing it into thick, steak-like pieces is even better. In this recipe, preheating the baking sheet is an important step to ensure a perfectly browned, crispy "steak." It is also ideal if you can find a head of cauliflower with a thick stalk, which will help hold everything together when you're slicing. After the cauliflower steaks are roasted, a delicious gremolata made from fresh parsley, lemon zest, garlic and oil is drizzled over the golden tops, resulting in a balanced side dish that would even work well as a vegetarian entrée.

SERVES **4**
HANDS-ON TIME: **10 MINUTES**
TOTAL TIME: **38 MINUTES**

1 large head cauliflower, stem trimmed

6 tablespoons extra-virgin olive oil

1 ¼ teaspoons kosher salt

¾ teaspoon black pepper

1 cup firmly packed fresh flat-leaf parsley leaves, finely chopped

1 ½ tablespoons lemon zest

1 garlic clove, finely chopped

1   Place a rimmed baking sheet in the oven, and preheat the oven to 450°F. (Do not remove the baking sheet while the oven preheats.) Carefully cut 4 (½-inch-thick) steaks vertically from the center of the cauliflower head; reserve the remaining cauliflower for another use. Drizzle both sides of the steaks with 1 ½ tablespoons of the oil; sprinkle with 1 teaspoon of the salt and ½ teaspoon of the pepper. Place the cauliflower in a single layer on the hot baking sheet, and return to the oven.

2   Bake the cauliflower steaks until the bottom sides are browned, about 14 minutes. Carefully turn the steaks over. Bake until the cauliflower is tender and browned on the other side, about 14 minutes more.

3   Stir together the parsley, lemon zest, garlic, 3 ½ tablespoons of the oil, and the remaining ¼ teaspoon each salt and pepper in a medium bowl. Serve the gremolata over the cauliflower steaks. Drizzle with the remaining 1 tablespoon olive oil.

Broccoli-Cheddar Fritters

SERVES **4**
HANDS-ON TIME: **25 MINUTES**
TOTAL TIME: **55 MINUTES**

Broccoli and Cheddar cheese go together like milk and cookies, like Sonny and Cher, like the sun and the moon, like mommies and wine? You get the picture. They are a terrific pair. The addition of gooey, creamy Cheddar on the healthy, green veggie is particularly helpful with picky eaters. In this recipe, a child might not even know he or she was eating broccoli, as it is finely chopped and mixed with cheese, flour, eggs and wonderful flavorings. Then it is formed into patties, sautéed in peanut oil until golden brown and served with a dollop of sour cream. It is a delicious side dish, and could even be bulked up with lettuce, tomatoes and condiments and served on a bun as a veggie burger. I think Broccoli famously put it best, "Cheddar cheese, you complete me."

1 pound fresh broccoli florets

1 cup shredded sharp Cheddar cheese

3 tablespoons all-purpose flour

4 large eggs, beaten

2 garlic cloves, chopped

3/4 teaspoon kosher salt

1/2 teaspoon black pepper

1/4 teaspoon cayenne pepper

1/3 cup peanut oil

1/4 cup sour cream

Lemon wedges (optional)

1 Pulse half of the broccoli in a food processor until finely chopped, about 10 times, and place in a large bowl. Repeat with the remaining broccoli. Add the cheese, flour, eggs, garlic, salt, black pepper, and cayenne to the broccoli, and stir to combine. Scoop the broccoli mixture by 1/2-cup portions, and place on a baking sheet, patting each into a 3 1/2-inch-wide patty. (You should have 8 patties.) Cover and chill for at least 30 minutes.

2 Heat the oil in a large skillet over medium-high. Cook the broccoli patties, 4 at a time, until golden brown, 3 to 4 minutes per side. Drain on paper towels. Serve with the sour cream and lemon wedges, if you like.

SIRIOUSLY VARIED

The veggie is interchangeable— try this with zucchini or spinach instead.

SIRIOUSLY MINI

Try making the patties smaller and serving them on little buns as sliders for the kids!

KALE SALAD

1 mini baguette, broken into pieces

2 tablespoons olive oil

1/4 teaspoon kosher salt

1/4 teaspoon black pepper

1 cup finely chopped prosciutto

4 ounces ricotta salata (about 1 cup)

1/2 cup pepperoncinis, stems removed

1/3 cup kalamata olives, pitted

10 cups thinly sliced black kale (Lacinato), stems removed (from 2 bunches)

1/2 cup cherry tomatoes, halved

1 large avocado, diced

DRESSING

(Makes 1 1/2 cups)

1 cup olive oil

1/4 cup red wine vinegar

1 tablespoon dried oregano

1/2 teaspoon kosher salt

1/4 teaspoon black pepper

Juice of 1 lemon

Kale and Avocado Salad with Crispy Breadcrumbs

Photograph on page 8

It seems people either love kale or hate kale, and if you find yourself in the latter category I swear this salad will change your mind. Carson and I ordered something similar at one of our favorite restaurants in California (Love & Salt in Manhattan Beach, if you must know), and I've been recreating it at home ever since. Once you give it a go, you'll want crispy breadcrumbs on everything. It gives each leafy bite a spectacular crunch, without having to stab at a clunky crouton. While curly, green kale is more common, the Lacinato black kale used here offers a richer flavor and a sturdier vessel for the rest of the ingredients to cling to. Most importantly, I like to chop everything as small as possible for easy-to-eat, uniform bites. Kale haters, try this, and then let us rejoice as kale lovers forevermore.

1 Make the Kale Salad: Place the pieces of the baguette in a food processor, and pulse until breadcrumbs have formed, about 3 times.

2 Heat the olive oil in a skillet over medium. Add the breadcrumbs, and cook until golden, stirring often, about 5 minutes. Sprinkle with the salt and pepper. Remove from the skillet, and set aside.

3 Add the prosciutto to the skillet, and cook over medium heat until crisp, 5 to 10 minutes. Remove from the heat, and set aside.

4 Process the ricotta salata, pepperoncinis, and olives in a food processor; pulse until small crumbles form, 3 to 4 times. Gently stir together the ricotta mixture, prosciutto, kale, tomatoes, avocado, and breadcrumbs in a bowl.

5 Make the Dressing: Pour the oil, vinegar, oregano, salt, pepper, and lemon juice into a mason jar. Cover with the lid, and shake until well combined (or you can whisk everything together in a bowl). Drizzle your desired amount of dressing on the salad—I used about 1/2 cup— and toss to coat.

Pan-Roasted Brussels Sprouts

Photograph on page 161

I was one of those kids who actually enjoyed Brussels sprouts. Every Thanksgiving I looked forward to the vegetable, which was usually steamed or sautéed, but then had to wait another year before eating it again. Nowadays, Brussels sprouts seem to be served year-round in many different ways, and I couldn't be happier about that. This is one of my favorite ways to enjoy the little leafy buds, most likely because once they are sautéed with fresh lemon, thyme and toasted breadcrumbs, they are sprinkled with salty, crispy prosciutto. Everything in life is better with salty, crispy prosciutto. Also, have I mentioned that you cook the prosciutto in the microwave? It is a SIRI-ously life-changing hack. No need to wait for Turkey Day to enjoy this delicious side dish!

1. Combine the Brussels sprouts, water, and oil in a large skillet; cover and bring to a boil over high. Boil until the Brussels sprouts are almost tender, about 5 minutes. Uncover and add the salt, pepper, and thyme, and cook until the Brussels sprouts are browned and the water is evaporated, 3 to 4 minutes. Stir in the lemon zest and juice. Sprinkle with the breadcrumbs.

2. Wrap the prosciutto in a paper towel in a single layer. Microwave on HIGH until crisp, about 2 minutes. Break into pieces, and sprinkle over the Brussels sprouts.

SERVES **4**

HANDS-ON TIME: **18 MINUTES**

TOTAL TIME: **18 MINUTES**

1 pound fresh Brussels sprouts, trimmed and halved

¼ cup water

3 tablespoons olive oil

1 teaspoon kosher salt

½ teaspoon black pepper

½ teaspoon chopped fresh thyme

½ teaspoon lemon zest plus 1 teaspoon fresh juice

¼ cup panko (Japanese-style breadcrumbs), toasted

2 ounces thinly sliced prosciutto

SIRIOUSLY **FANCY**

Shaving the sprouts with a sharp knife or mandoline (one of my favorite kitchen tools) is a great way to "fancy up" the dish.

SERVES **8**

HANDS-ON TIME: **10 MINUTES**

TOTAL TIME: **35 MINUTES**

2 medium zucchini

2 medium-sized yellow squash

3 tablespoons olive oil

1 ¼ teaspoons kosher salt

¾ teaspoon black pepper

1 ½ cups shredded Manchego cheese

1 cup panko (Japanese-style breadcrumbs)

Manchego Summer Squash Gratin

This might be one of the things I make that Carson requests the most. He grew up loving scalloped potatoes but nowadays doesn't always crave the heavy richness associated with that dish. Alternatively, this summer squash gratin is light, colorful, and just tender enough with a terrific crunch from the breadcrumbs. (I really sound like a mom when I say things like "terrific crunch," don't I?) The best part about this recipe is how quickly you can make it, especially if you have a mandoline. This handy kitchen tool easily slices your squash and zucchini into uniform circles and will also ensure that they cook evenly. It's a perfect summer side but also something we tend to make all year long.

1   Preheat the oven to 450°F with an oven rack about 8 inches from the heat. Using a mandoline or sharp knife, slice the zucchini and the yellow squash thinly on the bias into ¼-inch-thick slices. Toss with 2 tablespoons of the olive oil, 1 teaspoon of the salt, and ½ teaspoon of the pepper. Spread half of the squash mixture in a lightly greased, 11- x 7-inch baking dish. Sprinkle with ¾ cup of the cheese, and top with the remaining half of squash. Bake until tender, 15 to 20 minutes.

2   Meanwhile, stir together the panko and remaining ¾ cup cheese, 1 tablespoon olive oil, and ¼ teaspoon each salt and pepper. Remove the casserole from the oven, and sprinkle with the panko mixture. Return to the oven, and bake for 5 minutes. Increase the temperature to a high broil (do not remove the dish), and broil until the top is golden brown, 3 to 5 minutes.

Hello, Zucchini Police? I found the missing baby. This is normal.

Zucchini Linguini with Pistachio-and-Pea Pesto

SERVES **4**

HANDS-ON TIME: **15 MINUTES**

TOTAL TIME: **30 MINUTES**

Zucchini noodles, or "zoodles" as they're often called, are all the rage these days. You can find them precut in the grocery store (shortcut!), you can buy a vegetable spiralizer or you can use the method below, which only requires a vegetable peeler for flat, linguini-like noodles. However you zoodle it, they make a nutritious side dish that would be great served with just about any protein. In this recipe, the zucchini linguini (almost as fun to say as "zoodle") is served with a homemade pistachio-and-pea pesto. The flavors in the pesto take the otherwise mild zucchini to a new level with a fresh, nutty brightness that rivals any traditional linguini dish. ZOODLE! (You know, like BAM! Just go with it.)

4 large zucchini (skin left on or peeled off, depending on preference)

1 teaspoon kosher salt

½ cup raw, unsalted, shelled pistachios

½ cup frozen green peas, thawed

2 tablespoons grated Parmesan cheese, plus more for garnish

1 tablespoon chopped fresh basil

1 garlic clove

½ teaspoon black pepper

¾ cup plus 2 tablespoons olive oil

1 Using a vegetable peeler, peel the zucchini lengthwise to make long, flat "noodles." Once you see the seeds, turn the zucchini and repeat the process.

2 Place the zucchini noodles in a colander, sprinkle with ½ teaspoon of the salt, and let stand 15 to 20 minutes. Wrap the zucchini noodles in paper towels, and press to release the excess moisture.

3 Process the pistachios, peas, Parmesan, basil, garlic, and ¼ teaspoon each of the salt and pepper in a blender or food processor until well combined, about 5 seconds. With the blender running, pour ¾ cup of the olive oil in a slow, steady stream through the food chute, and process until smooth.

4 Heat the remaining 2 tablespoons olive oil in a large skillet over high, swirling to coat. Remove from the heat, and add the zucchini noodles to quickly heat through, stirring constantly, about 1 minute. Add ⅓ cup of the pesto and the remaining ¼ teaspoon each of the salt and pepper. Toss to coat; garnish with grated Parmesan, if desired.

SERVES **4**
HANDS-ON TIME: **15 MINUTES**
TOTAL TIME: **1 HOUR**
5 MINUTES

- **1 (3-pound) spaghetti squash, halved lengthwise, seeds removed**
- **¼ cup plus 1 tablespoon extra-virgin olive oil**
- **¼ teaspoon black pepper**
- **¾ teaspoon kosher salt**
- **4 garlic cloves, thinly sliced**
- **½ teaspoon crushed red pepper**
- **½ cup shredded Parmesan cheese**
- **Fresh basil leaves**

SIRIOUSLY MINI

Toss with marinara sauce and Parmesan for the kiddos.

Spaghetti Squash Aglio e Olio

Photograph on page 170

My father-in-law introduced me to Spaghetti Aglio e Olio, and it was love at first bite. As an Italian, he grew up with at least a small amount of pasta at every meal. I wish that were my story, but I am Midwest Dutch, and our meals came with a side of casserole and passive aggressiveness. Back to my father-in-law...who was a bear of a man with a heart of gold...when he was cooking his pasta dinners regularly, there was no getting in his way. I would always offer to help, but he was a cook on a mission. Spaghetti Aglio e Olio, which is basically pasta with olive oil, garlic and red pepper flakes, was always a staple at these dinners. I've since put my own twist on this dish by using spaghetti squash instead of pasta. It provides the same traditional flavors with a nutritious, mildly-sweet vegetable base. In memory of Pops, however, I might always need to make a little of both...there is no tricking an Italian into thinking squash is pasta.

1 Preheat the oven to 400°F. Drizzle the cut sides of the spaghetti squash with 1 tablespoon of the olive oil; sprinkle with the pepper and ½ teaspoon of the salt. Place the squash, cut sides down, on a rimmed baking sheet. Bake until the squash is tender, 35 to 40 minutes. Cool on a baking sheet for 15 minutes. Scrape the inside of the squash with a fork to remove the spaghetti-like strands, and place them in a bowl.

2 Heat the garlic, red pepper, and the remaining ¼ cup of oil and ¼ teaspoon of salt in a large skillet over medium. Cook, stirring often, until the garlic is light brown, 3 to 4 minutes. Add the spaghetti squash and cook, stirring often, until heated through, about 4 minutes. Sprinkle with the Parmesan, and garnish with basil leaves.

Sautéed Spinach with Browned Butter

Photograph on page 173

Am I the only one who grew up associating spinach with Popeye the Sailor Man? As a child, the mere mention of the vegetable would make my skin crawl. Why must I eat something green just because it makes a bald man grow muscles? Now that I'm much, MUCH older (because half of you are probably like, Popeye Who?), I've come to love the leafy green...in salads, in smoothies, in creamy dips, and especially sautéed in brown butter. When you brown butter, a lovely, nutty aroma is released, and this pairs so nicely with the earthy flavor of spinach. A hint of nutmeg and lots of fresh garlic lend to the delicious tastes this healthy side dish has to offer. Your taste buds and muscles alike will agree.

1   Melt the butter in a small skillet over medium. Add the nutmeg and ½ teaspoon of the salt, and cook, stirring occasionally, until any foam subsides and the butter turns light golden brown, about 4 minutes. Pour into a small bowl, and set aside.

2   Heat the olive oil in a large skillet over medium. Add the garlic, pepper, half of the spinach, and the remaining 1 teaspoon of salt. Cook, stirring often, until the spinach reduces in volume, about 2 minutes. Add the remaining spinach and cook, stirring often, until wilted, 1 to 2 minutes. Transfer to a warm serving platter, and drizzle with the browned butter.

SERVES **4**
HANDS-ON TIME: **10 MINUTES**
TOTAL TIME: **10 MINUTES**

½ cup unsalted butter

⅛ teaspoon ground nutmeg

1 ½ teaspoons kosher salt

2 tablespoons olive oil

4 garlic cloves, chopped

½ teaspoon black pepper

1 (10-ounce) package fresh baby spinach

SIRIOUSLY FANCY

Freshly grated nutmeg will assist in creating a wonderful depth of flavor in this dish.

Monica's Spanish Beans

SERVES **4**
HANDS-ON TIME: **10 MINUTES**
TOTAL TIME: **10 MINUTES**

This is a simple yet hearty side dish that has a depth of flavors from salty bacon, tangy tomato sauce and fresh cilantro. The real star of this recipe is a flavorful ingredient called sofrito, which is a sauce made of garlic, onions, peppers, tomatoes and spices, and is used as a base for many Spanish dishes. A family friend, Monica, makes her own, which is why this recipe is named after her. However, you can purchase sofrito in the store, and then these can be your beans. Sharing is caring, after all. I highly recommend trying it out and serving them with rice the next time you make pork chops or skirt steak.

1 tablespoon vegetable oil

1 bacon slice, diced

1 tablespoon jarred sofrito (such as Goya)

½ cup tomato sauce

1 teaspoon white vinegar

1 (15-ounce) can red kidney beans, undrained

2 tablespoons chopped fresh cilantro

Hot cooked long-grain white rice (optional)

1   Heat the oil in a skillet over medium. Add the diced bacon, and cook, stirring often, until crispy, about 4 minutes.

2   Stir in the sofrito, and cook until heated through, about 1 minute.

3   Add the tomato sauce and vinegar, and cook until the mixture begins to bubble, about 2 minutes.

4   Once bubbling, stir in the can of beans. Bring to a boil; reduce the heat to medium-low, and cover. Simmer until the beans are soft and cooked through, about 2 minutes.

5   Sprinkle with the chopped cilantro. Serve with rice, if desired.

Sweet Treats

We have something called "Treat Nights" at our house, which are scheduled for Monday, Wednesday, Friday and Saturday evenings. Why do we limit ourselves to just four nights, you wonder? The answer is simple: We are Treatoholics. We require moderation. No, seriously, my daughter Etta even wants to change her name to Etta Candy. Our passion for dessert is so strong, that even nontreat nights have evolved into something like teeny-tiny-treat nights (example: a few chocolate chips). It simply feels so pleasing—and necessary in our case—to end the day with something sweet.

I am probably to blame for this obsession. Some of my fondest childhood memories involve baking with my mom and grandmother during the holidays, on special occasions or for no reason at all. One of my proudest moments was the first time I made my own batch of cookies from scratch, following the recipe on the back of a chocolate chip bag. Sometimes, I would create homemade "candy bars" (melting chocolate into ice cube trays...fancy stuff). Basically, my devotion to desserts started off strong and has only grown since. At times, it is actually baffling to me that I'm the mom baking in the kitchen now, creating memories with my own children.

While we are a treat-loving family, Carson and I have very different palates when it comes to enjoying sugary foods. He is into light, fluffy cakes with fruit and whipped toppings, banana puddings, peanut butter and caramel ice creams and root beer gummies (random). Me? Chocolate. Anything chocolate. Everything chocolate. The richer the better. Therefore, in order to please everyone, I have developed an impressive repertoire of baked goods. And even though I am a chocolate girl, quite honestly, I have only met one dessert that I didn't like: pumpkin pie. Look elsewhere if you need a recipe for that bad boy.

What you will find in this chapter, however, is a diverse collection of mouthwatering, delectable desserts that are simple and straightforward. I'm not going to make you sift your flour or temper your chocolate. No one wants to do those things! (Also, I do not know how to temper chocolate.) Instead, whip up an easy batch of delicious Cookie Butter Truffles or Vanilla Bean Sugar Cookies. If you have a little more time, you will impress anyone with my life-altering Homemade Tagalong Cookies or the Chocolate Dream Layer Cake. There are even treats in here that sneak in some fruits and veggies! Win win!

Whatever you decide on, I hope you enjoy these sweets as much as we do. Any one of them will be perfect for your next "Treat Night" which is, let's be honest, every night of the week.

2 cups powdered sugar

1 cup creamy cookie butter (such as Biscoff)

½ cup unsalted butter, softened

¼ teaspoon vanilla extract

1 (12-ounce) package semisweet chocolate chips

1 tablespoon vegetable oil

Toppings of your choice such as crushed cookies or candy sprinkles

SIRIOUSLY IMPORTANT

Be sure to chill the dough balls before dipping them into the chocolate sauce so that they keep their shape.

Cookie Butter Truffles

I have always loved making my own truffles. There is something very therapeutic about rolling out each perfectly imperfect ball of confection. A traditional truffle is made with rich chocolate ganache, but the varietal possibilities are endless. Cookie Butter, which is a rich, sweet spread made from biscuit cookies, makes a delectable truffle interior. It is mixed with powdered sugar, butter and vanilla, rolled into balls and dipped in semisweet chocolate. These make an excellent edible gift around the holidays. I dare you to name a person who wouldn't enjoy a box of homemade Cookie Butter Truffles. Now you have all the teachers and friendly neighbors in your life covered...you're welcome.

1   Beat the powdered sugar, cookie butter, butter, and vanilla with an electric mixer on medium-low speed until creamy, about 3 minutes.

2   Scoop about 1 tablespoon of the dough, and, using your hands, form into a 1-inch ball, rolling with your hands to smooth. Place on a large parchment paper-lined baking sheet. Repeat with the remaining dough. Chill for 15 minutes.

3   Combine the chocolate and oil in a small saucepan over low. Cook, stirring constantly, until melted and well combined, 3 to 4 minutes. Remove from the heat.

4   Using two forks, dip each ball into the melted chocolate, letting any excess chocolate drip back into the pan. Return the dipped balls to a parchment paper-lined baking sheet.

5   Sprinkle with toppings, and chill until firm, about 15 minutes.

Perfect Salted Chocolate Chip Cookies

MAKES **ABOUT 36**
HANDS-ON TIME: **20 MINUTES**
TOTAL TIME: **1 HOUR**
15 MINUTES

I should admit that I have probably made 78 versions of the infamous chocolate chip cookie in my lifetime, each one distinct. Sometimes I brown the butter for flavor, often I use bread or cake flour for texture, and there is always the possibility I will mess around with how much or what kind of chocolate I add. Over time, however, I have perfected my method and, in turn, developed an ideal cookie: soft and chewy in the center with slightly crisp edges. The chilled dough ensures a flawless cookie shape, and most importantly, each one is sprinkled with flaky sea salt. Chocolate and salt create magic, period. Memorize this recipe, and you won't be sorry.

1 cup unsalted butter, softened

³/₄ cup granulated sugar

1 cup packed light brown sugar

2 large eggs, at room temperature

1 ½ teaspoons vanilla extract

2 ½ cups all-purpose flour

³/₄ teaspoon baking soda

1 teaspoon baking powder

½ teaspoon table salt

1 ½ (12-ounce) packages bittersweet chocolate chips

1 tablespoon flaky sea salt (such as Maldon)

1 Beat the butter and both sugars in a stand mixer on medium speed until creamy, about 2 minutes. Add the eggs and vanilla, beating until combined.

2 Combine the flour, baking soda, baking powder, and table salt in a small bowl. Gradually add to the butter mixture, beating just until blended after each addition. Beat in the chocolate chips just until combined. Chill the dough for 30 minutes.

3 Preheat the oven to 350°F. Drop the chilled dough, by tablespoonfuls, 2 inches apart onto parchment paper-lined baking sheets. Sprinkle the cookies evenly with the sea salt.

4 Bake until the cookies reach your desired degree of doneness, about 12 minutes for a medium-soft cookie. Transfer the cookies to wire racks, and cool completely, about 15 minutes.

MAKES **36**
HANDS-ON TIME: **10 MINUTES**
TOTAL TIME: **1 HOUR**

2 ripe bananas

¹/₂ cup unsalted butter, softened

¹/₂ cup creamy peanut butter

¹/₂ cup packed dark brown sugar

1 teaspoon vanilla extract

1 large egg

¹/₂ cup plus ¹/₄ cup granulated sugar

2 cups all-purpose flour

¹/₂ teaspoon baking powder

¹/₂ teaspoon baking soda

¹/₄ teaspoon kosher salt

1 teaspoon ground cinnamon

1 cup semisweet chocolate chips

Chocolate Chip-Peanut Butter-Banana Cookies

For Your Information! This was probably the first recipe that I developed on my blog that started generating feedback. Prior to this creation, I was certain only my mom was reading my online, food-related ramblings. It was a pleasant surprise to realize that people were not only reading, they were trying out my recipes and enjoying them. Now, I'm a cookbook author (what?!?), but I still have a soft spot for this sweet treat. Literally. These cookies are very cake-like in consistency. I would describe them as delicate, pillow-y fluffs of cookie goodness. Do I sound like a cookbook author yet? They are extremely flavorful and would make great after-school treats for the kiddos, or yourself.

1 Mash the bananas in a large bowl. Add the butter, peanut butter, brown sugar, vanilla, egg, and ¹/₂ cup of the granulated sugar. Stir to combine.

2 Whisk together the flour, baking powder, baking soda, salt, and ¹/₂ teaspoon of the cinnamon. Add the flour mixture to the banana mixture, and stir to combine.

3 Stir in the chocolate chips. Cover with plastic wrap, and chill for 30 minutes.

4 Preheat the oven to 350°F. Combine the remaining ¹/₄ cup granulated sugar and ¹/₂ teaspoon cinnamon in a small bowl.

5 Drop the chilled dough by tablespoonfuls, 2 inches apart, onto parchment paper-lined baking sheets. Sprinkle with the cinnamon-sugar mixture.

6 Bake until the cookies are golden brown and just set, about 10 minutes. Cool the cookies on the pans for 10 minutes. Transfer the cookies to wire racks, and try to let them cool some more before devouring.

MAKES **42**

HANDS-ON TIME: **1 HOUR**

TOTAL TIME: **2 HOURS**
10 MINUTES

COOKIES

1 cup unsalted butter, at room temperature

½ cup powdered sugar

½ teaspoon vanilla extract

⅛ teaspoon almond extract

2 cups all-purpose flour

½ teaspoon table salt

COCONUT-CARAMEL TOPPING

2 ½ cups sweetened shredded coconut

12 ounces store-bought caramel candies

2 tablespoons whole milk

Pinch of table salt

CHOCOLATE COATING

6 ounces milk chocolate baking bar, chopped

6 ounces semisweet or dark chocolate baking bar, chopped

1 teaspoon vegetable oil

SIRIOUSLY **SIMPLE**

If your caramel sauce gets too stiff while cooking, simply stir in 1 to 2 tablespoons of cream to soften it up again.

Homemade Samoas

Two things have remained memorable from my time as a Girl Scout (or Brownie, rather) and those are the hideous, uncomfortable, brown pants I wore when everyone else in my troop wore skirts, and, of course, selling cookies. The latter—being a positive memory—inspired me to make my own version of their popular treats. Samoas, or Caramel deLites as they're also called, were my favorite Girl Scout cookie. What's not to love about rich, buttery shortbread topped with a creamy, coconut-caramel sauce and drizzled with sweet chocolate? These look and taste amazingly close to the real deal; honestly, you could probably try selling them. Just make sure to wear the outfit.

1   Preheat the oven to 300°F.

2   **Make the Cookies:** Beat the butter and powdered sugar with an electric mixer on medium speed until smooth. Add the vanilla and almond extracts, and beat until combined.

3   Sift together the flour and salt in a separate bowl. Slowly add the sifted ingredients to the butter mixture, beating on low speed until combined. Shape the dough into a disk; wrap in plastic wrap, and chill 30 minutes.

4   **Meanwhile, Make the Topping:** Spread the coconut on a baking sheet. Bake until lightly toasted, about 10 minutes, stirring frequently. (Be careful, as coconut burns easily!) Set aside. Increase the oven temperature to 350°F.

5   Unwrap the chilled dough disk, and roll it out on a lightly floured surface to a ¼-inch thickness. Cut the dough, using a floured 2-inch round cutter. Using the tip of a sharp knife, cut out a ¾-inch circle in the center of each cookie, reserving the cutouts for scraps. (I use the small round tip of a pastry tube to cut out the inner circle.) Reroll the scraps as necessary. Place the cookies, 1 inch apart, on parchment paper-lined baking sheets.

6   Bake until the edges begin to slightly brown, 10 to 12 minutes. Cool the cookies on the pans for 5 minutes, then transfer to wire racks, and let cool completely, about 20 minutes.

7   For the Coconut-Caramel Topping, place the caramels, milk, and salt in a saucepan over low, and cook, stirring occasionally, until melted and smooth. Stir in the toasted coconut, and remove from the heat.

8   Spread the topping over the top of each cooled cookie. (I found the easiest method is to cover the entire cookie, and then stick the tip of my knife through the hole to remove the topping in the center.) Let stand until the topping is set, about 20 minutes.

9 Meanwhile, Make the Chocolate Coating: Pour water to a depth of 1 inch into the bottom of a double boiler over medium; bring to a boil. Reduce the heat to a simmer; place the chocolate in the top of the double boiler (or place a heat-proof bowl over simmering water, making sure the water does not touch the bowl), and stir until melted. Add the vegetable oil, and stir until you have a glossy chocolate sauce. Remove from the heat.

10 Dip the bottoms of the caramel-covered cookies into the Chocolate Coating by holding each cookie between your thumb and pointer finger. Place on parchment paper-lined baking sheets.

11 Place the remaining Chocolate Coating in a piping bag, a ziplock plastic bag with the corner snipped off, or a plastic condiment squeeze bottle. Drizzle the chocolate over the top of each cookie. Chill the cookies until firm and set, about 15 minutes.

Homemade Tagalongs

In my house, the chocolate/peanut butter combination tends to trump all. Luckily for my family, my second favorite Girl Scout cookie has always been Tagalongs. They have a smooth, chocolate exterior and the inside is luscious peanut butter cream on top of crisp shortbread. For this reason, I created a homemade version of the hit cookie and they are truly magical. I would even be so bold as to say they are better than the real thing, because they are made with love. Is that a cheesy thing to say? I don't care. While these might be more time consuming than your average homemade cookie, the best part about them is how many they yield. Once you're finished, you can eat what's equivalent to "a sleeve" of cookies, which is totally not something I've ever done before, box after box...

COOKIES

1 cup unsalted butter, at room temperature

½ cup powdered sugar

½ teaspoon vanilla extract

⅛ teaspoon almond extract

2 cups all-purpose flour

½ teaspoon table salt

PEANUT BUTTER FILLING

¾ cup creamy peanut butter

½ cup powdered sugar

¼ teaspoon vanilla extract

Pinch of table salt

CHOCOLATE COATING

6 ounces milk chocolate baking bar, chopped

6 ounces semisweet or dark chocolate baking bar, chopped

1 teaspoon vegetable oil

SIRIOUSLY SIMPLE

If you don't have a double boiler, place a heat-proof bowl over simmering water, making sure the water does not touch the bowl.

---

1   Make the Cookies: Beat the butter and powdered sugar with an electric mixer on medium speed until smooth, about 4 minutes. Add the vanilla and almond extracts, and beat until combined.

2   Sift together the flour and salt in a separate bowl. Slowly add the flour mixture to the butter mixture, beating on low speed until combined.

3   Shape the dough into a disk; wrap in plastic wrap, and chill for 30 minutes.

4   Preheat the oven to 350°F. Unwrap the chilled dough disk, and roll it out on a lightly floured surface to a ¼-inch thickness. Cut the dough using a floured 2-inch round cutter, rerolling scraps once. Place the cookies 1 inch apart on parchment paper-lined baking sheets.

5   Bake until the edges just begin to turn golden, 12 to 14 minutes. Cool the cookies on the pans for 5 minutes, then transfer to wire racks, and let cool completely, about 20 minutes.

6   Meanwhile, Make the Peanut Butter Filling: Beat the peanut butter, sugar, vanilla, and salt on medium speed until well combined.

7   Mound about 1 teaspoon of the filling on top of each cooled cookie. Using a knife and starting in the middle of the mound, spread the filling down to the edge of the cookie. Repeat as you go around the cookie until the filling covers the entire top. The filling should look slightly domed in the center of the cookie. (There will be about ¼ cup filling leftover.)

8   Make the Chocolate Coating: Pour water to a depth of 1 inch into the bottom of a double boiler over medium; bring to a boil. Reduce the heat to a simmer; place the chocolate in the top of the double boiler, and stir until melted. Add the vegetable oil, and stir until you have a glossy chocolate sauce. Remove from the heat.

9   Using 2 forks, dip each cookie into the coating until the cookie is completely coated on both sides, flipping over, if necessary. Lift the cookie out of the chocolate with 1 fork, using the other to scrape any excess chocolate off the bottom back into the pan. Place on aluminum foil- or parchment paper-lined baking sheets. Repeat with the remaining cookies and Chocolate Coating.

10 Chill the cookies until firm, about 15 minutes. Store leftovers (if you have any!) in an airtight container in the refrigerator to help them keep their shape.

Vanilla Bean Sugar Cookies

I'm guilty of trying to put chocolate in every cookie I bake. Peanut butter, snickerdoodle, oatmeal...to me, chocolate chips make them all that much better. A good sugar cookie, however, is where I draw the line. The creamy blend of butter and granulated sugar is all that a sugar cookie needs to shine. In this recipe, however, the addition of vanilla bean paste makes them truly shine...bright like a diamond (Rihanna even wrote a song about it). The sweet flecks of vanilla beans speckle each cookie in such a pretty, delightful way. They are tender on the inside with crisp edges, and they would be perfect dipped in ice cream or dunked in coffee. No chocolate necessary, and that's saying a lot coming from me.

1 Beat the sugar and butter with an electric mixer on medium-high speed until light and fluffy, about 3 minutes. Scrape down the sides with a spatula. Add the egg and vanilla bean paste, and beat until combined.

2 Whisk together the flour, baking powder, salt, and baking soda. Add half of the flour mixture to the butter mixture; beat on low speed until just combined.

3 Beat in the sour cream until just combined. Add the remaining flour mixture, and beat until a dough forms. Cover with plastic wrap, and chill for 30 minutes.

4 Meanwhile, preheat the oven to 350°F.

5 Using a 1½-inch cookie scoop, form the chilled dough into 24 balls. (They will be about the size of golf balls.) If desired, dip 1 side of the dough ball in sanding sugar or candy sprinkles. Place the cookies (sugar-side up, if using) on parchment paper-lined baking sheets, 2 inches apart.

6 Bake until the edges start to slightly brown, 10 to 15 minutes. Cool the cookies on the pans for 10 minutes. Transfer to wire racks, and let cool.

MAKES 24
HANDS-ON TIME: 10 MINUTES
TOTAL TIME: 1 HOUR
5 MINUTES

1½ cups granulated sugar

1 cup unsalted butter, at room temperature

1 large egg

1½ teaspoons vanilla bean paste

2½ cups all-purpose flour

1 teaspoon baking powder

½ teaspoon kosher salt

¼ teaspoon baking soda

¼ cup sour cream

Sanding sugar or candy sprinkles (optional)

SIRIOUSLY VARIED

If you do not have vanilla bean paste on hand, swap with the same amount of vanilla extract.

MAKES **20**
HANDS-ON TIME: **10 MINUTES**
TOTAL TIME: **55 MINUTES**

½ cup unsalted butter

1 cup all-purpose flour

¼ teaspoon baking soda

¼ teaspoon baking powder

⅛ teaspoon kosher salt

1 cup packed dark brown sugar

1 ripe banana, mashed

1 teaspoon vanilla extract

1 large egg

½ cup hazelnut-chocolate spread
(such as Nutella)

Flaky sea salt (optional)

Browned Butter–Banana-Nutella Bars

I'm pretty certain my kids think Nutella is a food group. If it were up to them, it would be spread on everything and anything...toast, vegetables, toothbrushes. Good thing I am the boss and they have no say in their lives (#futuretherapy). Although I limit their intake of the chocolate-hazelnut spread, I cannot resist baking with it every once in awhile. Especially when browned butter and bananas are involved. Nutella and caramelized, nutty brown butter go hand in hand, and once both things unite with sweet bananas, the result is exquisite. These taste like a cross between chocolaty banana bread and blondies. They are very easy to whip up, so you're left with plenty of time to boss around your loved ones. Enjoy!

1   Preheat the oven to 350°F. Melt the butter in a small saucepan over medium-low, and cook until browned and foamy with a nutty aroma, 10 to 12 minutes. (Be careful not to burn the butter.) Remove from the heat, and let cool.

2   Whisk together the flour, baking soda, baking powder, and salt in a small bowl.

3   Stir together the browned butter and brown sugar in a medium bowl until just combined. Add the mashed banana, vanilla, and egg, and stir until just combined. Add the flour mixture, and stir until just combined.

4   Grease a 20 (2-inch) square compartment bar pan (as pictured) or 1 (8-inch) square baking dish. Drop the batter by tablespoonfuls into the bar pan compartments or spoon the batter into the baking dish. Add about 1 teaspoon Nutella to the batter in each bar pan compartment and swirl with a knife. Alternatively, dollop Nutella around the top of the batter in the baking dish and swirl with a knife. Sprinkle with sea salt, if desired.

5   Bake until golden brown and a wooden pick inserted into the center comes out clean, 10 to 12 minutes for the bar pan and 30 to 35 minutes for the baking dish. Transfer the pan to a wire rack, and let cool completely, 20 to 30 minutes, before slicing or removing from the pan.

MAKES **24**
HANDS-ON TIME: **20 MINUTES**
TOTAL TIME: **2 HOURS**
40 MINUTES

2 ³/₄ cups plus ²/₃ cup all-purpose flour

¹/₂ cup powdered sugar, plus more for dusting

¹/₂ cup unsalted butter, at room temperature

4 gingersnap cookies, crushed

¹/₄ teaspoon table salt

2 cups granulated sugar

6 large eggs

2 teaspoons lemon zest plus 1 cup fresh juice (from about 10 lemons)

SIRIOUSLY VARIED

You can swap Biscoff cookies for the gingersnaps for the same yummy result.

SIRIOUSLY IMPORTANT

Be sure to pour the custard mixture over the hot crust as soon as it's out of the oven, as this will help set the eggs and prevent the bars from inverting.

Lemon Bars

Photograph on page 222

These lemon bars are dreamy. From the buttery, lightly spiced shortbread crust to the creamy, custard curd filling...they are simply out of this world. To me, lemon bars paint a picture of a warm, summer afternoon, somewhere in the South, on a wide porch, with a breeze in the air, pitchers of cold iced tea on a table, and platters of lemon bars. Utopian, right? Should I turn this into a romance novel? No, okay. This sweet treat practically erupts with tart, lemon flavor, as any good lemon bar should. The filling is just set enough while still maintaining a lovely ooey-gooey-ness. While it may be true that I daydream about enjoying these on the set of *Gone with the Wind,* I confess that these Lemon Bars are perfect anywhere and anytime.

1   Preheat the oven to 350°F. Line a 13- x 9-inch glass baking dish with parchment paper, allowing 2 to 3 inches to extend over sides. Place 2 ³/₄ cups of the flour in a large bowl, and stir in the ¹/₂ cup powdered sugar. Add the butter, cookie crumbs, and salt, and use your hands to incorporate the mixture into a crumbly but smooth dough. Pat into an even layer in the prepared baking dish. Freeze for 15 minutes, then transfer to the oven, and bake until golden brown, 15 to 20 minutes.

2   Meanwhile, whisk together the granulated sugar and eggs until well combined. Whisk in the lemon zest and juice. Whisk in the remaining ²/₃ cup flour until smooth. Pour the mixture over the hot crust; return to the oven, and bake until set but the mixture still moves together as a unit when lightly shaken, 20 to 25 minutes. Remove from the oven, and cool on a wire rack for 30 minutes.

3   Run a paring knife along the edges of the cooled baking dish to loosen the parchment, if needed. Using the parchment handles, lift the bars out of the baking dish. Cool completely on a wire rack, about 1 hour.

4   Using a sharp knife, cut the bars into 24 squares. Dust with powdered sugar just before serving.

Zucchini Brownies

Photograph on page 222

Once upon a time, a friend came to visit with a bounty of fresh produce from her garden. Amongst the fruits and vegetables were some giant zucchinis, and when I say giant I mean the size of human infants. I cooked with zucchini for days making soups, pastas, casseroles and yummy breads. Of course my picky children were having none of it, until it occurred to me that I could sneak the green veggie into brownies. Genius! These bars are cake-like in texture with a rich, fudgy ganache topping. Chocolate on top of chocolate helps distract from the fact that these brownies actually have some nutritional value. Now go forth, and fool your friends and family! The End.

1 Preheat the oven to 350°F. Place the chocolate in a small microwavable bowl, and microwave on HIGH until melted and smooth, about 1 minute and 30 seconds, stirring at 30-second intervals. Set aside.

2 Beat the sugar and butter with a stand mixer on medium speed until light and fluffy, about 4 minutes. Add the eggs, 1 at a time, beating just until blended after each addition. Stir together the flour, cocoa, baking powder, and salt. Add to the butter mixture alternately with the milk. Beat at low speed just until blended after each addition.

3 Squeeze the zucchini between paper towels to remove as much moisture as possible. Stir the zucchini, melted chocolate, and vanilla into the batter until well blended. Spoon the batter into a well greased (with shortening) 13- x 9-inch pan.

4 Bake until a wooden pick inserted in the center comes out clean, about 35 minutes. Cool completely on a wire rack, about 1 hour.

5 When the brownies are cooled, Make the Rich Fudge Ganache: Combine all the ingredients in a medium saucepan over medium-low. Cook, stirring often, until just melted and smooth, about 5 minutes. Spread immediately over the cooled brownies. Chill until the ganache is set, about 2 hours. Cut into 16 squares.

MAKES **16**
HANDS-ON TIME: **20 MINUTES**
TOTAL TIME: **3 HOURS 55 MINUTES**

---

1 (4-ounce) semisweet chocolate baking bar, finely chopped

2 cups granulated sugar

1 cup unsalted butter, softened

2 large eggs

2 cups all-purpose flour

2/3 cup unsweetened cocoa

1/2 teaspoon baking powder

1/2 teaspoon table salt

1/2 cup whole milk

2 cups finely shredded unpeeled zucchini

2 teaspoons vanilla extract

Vegetable shortening

RICH FUDGE GANACHE

3 (4-ounce) semisweet chocolate baking bars, finely chopped

6 tablespoons unsalted butter

1/4 cup heavy cream

SIRIOUSLY SIMPLE

Use the small holes of a box grater to get the perfect zucchini consistency for baking. Two medium zucchini yield about two cups.

SIRIOUSLY MINI

Try crumbling the brownies to make messy ice cream sundae toppings.

Zucchini
Brownies
PG 221

Lemon Bars
PG 220

Dark Chocolate–Mint Brownies with Chocolate Glaze

MAKES **16**
HANDS-ON TIME: **15 MINUTES**
TOTAL TIME: **2 HOURS**
22 MINUTES

Is there anything better than a holiday tradition? Nope, the answer is nope. Okay maybe there is something, and that is a Dark Chocolate–Mint Brownie with Chocolate Glaze. Every Christmas, my mom would make a version of these rich, minty bars—along with a slew of other treats—and one bite brings me back to our messy, festive kitchen. We would make batch after batch and hand them out as holiday gifts, which is something I still do today. Yes, maybe we all get bombarded with sweets during the season, but I love collecting those tins of homemade goodies to see what everyone else's traditions are. (Hint: Send me baked goods.) These bars begin with a fudgy brownie base, then are layered with creamy, cool mint and topped off with a chocolate glaze and crumbly mint candies. They are the perfect dessert for a jolly, memorable winter day.

¾ cup unsalted butter

1 (4-ounce) bittersweet chocolate baking bar, chopped

½ cup granulated sugar

½ cup packed light brown sugar

3 large eggs, lightly beaten

1 tablespoon vanilla extract

1 cup all-purpose flour

½ cup unsweetened cocoa

¼ teaspoon table salt

1 cup semisweet chocolate chips

MINT LAYER

1 ½ cups powdered sugar

3 tablespoons unsalted butter, melted

1 ½ tablespoons whole milk

½ teaspoon peppermint extract

CHOCOLATE GLAZE

1 (6-ounce) package semisweet chocolate chips

¼ cup heavy cream

16 thin crème de menthe chocolate mints (such as Andes), chopped (about ¾ cup)

1 Preheat the oven to 350°F. Line an 8-inch square baking pan with heavy-duty aluminum foil allowing 3 inches to extend over 2 sides; lightly grease the foil with cooking spray.

2 Melt the butter and chopped chocolate in a large saucepan over low. Stir in the sugars, eggs, and vanilla. Stir together the flour, cocoa, and salt in a bowl; stir into the chocolate mixture. Stir in the chocolate chips. Spoon the batter into the prepared pan.

3 Bake until a wooden pick inserted in the center comes out clean, 22 to 24 minutes. Cool completely in the pan on a wire rack, about 45 minutes.

4 Meanwhile, Make the Mint Layer: Combine all the ingredients in a medium bowl, and beat with an electric mixer on medium speed until smooth, about 1 minute. Spread over the cooled brownies. Chill for 1 hour.

5 Make the Chocolate Glaze: Place the chocolate chips and cream in a small microwavable bowl, and microwave on MEDIUM (50% power) until melted and smooth, 2 to 3 minutes, stirring at 30-second intervals. Spread over the Mint Layer. Sprinkle with the chopped mints. Chill until ready to serve.

6 Remove from the pan using the foil sides as handles. Cut into 16 squares.

MAKES **27**
HANDS-ON TIME: **40 MINUTES**
TOTAL TIME: **13 HOURS
40 MINUTES**

2 (14-ounce) containers dulce de leche ice cream, softened

1 cup coarsely chopped dry-roasted, salted peanuts (some left as halves)

1 (7-ounce) jar marshmallow creme

1 cup creamy peanut butter

½ teaspoon vanilla extract

1 (12-ounce) jar hot caramel ice cream topping

6 (4-ounce) semisweet chocolate baking bars, chopped

1 tablespoon vegetable shortening

SIRIOUSLY **VARIED**

While I love the warm sweetness that the dulce de leche brings to these bars, there is a great opportunity here to play with ice cream flavors. Cookies and cream, plain vanilla, chocolate, maybe even butter pecan or coffee...all could be good alternatives.

Homemade Frozen Snickers Bar

My favorite thing about these frozen bars—other than how similar they are to the actual thing—is the contrast in textures. The chocolate outer shell is nice and crispy, the caramel is gooey and creamy, the marshmallow nougat is thick and chewy, the ice cream is chilly and smooth and of course the peanuts are nice and crunchy. Combined, a palate-pleasing balance is achieved that is second only to the heavenly flavor. They possess the familiar, irresistible sweet and salty blend that Snickers candy is so famous for. Don't let how long these take scare you away—yes, 13 hours is like, half a day (I'm good at math)—but most of that time is spent letting the layers freeze and set. While that's happening, you can plan how you're going to impress your loved ones with this amazing frozen treat.

1 Line a 9-inch square pan with heavy-duty aluminum foil, allowing 3 inches to extend over 2 sides. Lightly grease the foil with cooking spray. Spread the ice cream in an even layer in the prepared pan. Sprinkle with ½ cup of the peanuts. Freeze for 2 hours.

2 Stir together the marshmallow creme, peanut butter, vanilla, and remaining ½ cup peanuts in a small bowl. Spread the mixture over the frozen ice cream. Cover and freeze for at least 2 hours.

3 Pour the caramel topping over the peanut butter mixture, and spread to smooth. Cover and freeze for 8 to 12 hours.

4 Remove the frozen ice cream mixture, using the aluminum-foil handles. Working quickly, use a hot knife to cut into 3 x 1-inch bars. Place the bars on a wire rack set in a rimmed baking sheet, and keep frozen while preparing the melted chocolate.

5 Place the chopped chocolate and shortening in a medium microwavable bowl, and microwave on HIGH until melted and smooth, 1 ½ to 2 minutes, stirring at 30-second intervals.

6 Spoon or pour the melted chocolate evenly over the frozen bars, coating the tops and sides. Return to the freezer, and freeze for at least 1 hour or up to 24 hours.

SERVES **24**

HANDS-ON TIME: **20 MINUTES**

TOTAL TIME: **1 HOUR 30 MINUTES**

2 cups water

1 ³/₄ cups granulated sugar

5 ounces bittersweet baking chocolate, chopped

½ cup unsalted butter

2 cups plus 2 tablespoons all-purpose flour

2 teaspoons baking powder

1 teaspoon baking soda

¼ teaspoon table salt

2 large eggs, lightly beaten

1 teaspoon pure vanilla extract

¼ cup fine graham cracker crumbs (about 3 sheets)

4 graham cracker sheets, roughly crumbled into large chunks

¼ cup packed light brown sugar

3 tablespoons unsalted butter, melted

³/₄ cup miniature marshmallows

2 (1.55-ounce) milk chocolate candy bars, each broken into 12 pieces

S'more Cupcakes

Photograph on page 230

It's hard to improve on a traditional s'more. In theory, what can be better than the simple yet infamous marshmallow, chocolate and graham cracker sandwich? I'll tell you what...these S'More Cupcakes! (I'm a fan of obvious transitions.) These moist, mini chocolate cakes are light and airy, and make the perfect vessel for everything on top. During the baking process, two layers are added to the cupcakes: first, a crumbly, buttery graham cracker streusel and second, a sticky, golden marshmallow topping. At last, they are finished off with a piece of milk chocolate. They are beautifully messy, and the perfect mouth-watering, Instagram-worthy cupcakes to upgrade your next campfire gathering with. Kumbaya!

1 Preheat the oven to 350°F. Line 2 (12-cup) standard-sized muffin pans with paper baking cups; coat with baking spray.

2 Combine the water and granulated sugar in a medium saucepan. Cook over medium-high, stirring occasionally, until the sugar dissolves completely, about 3 minutes. Remove from the heat, and stir in the bittersweet chocolate and ½ cup unsalted butter. Let stand for 10 minutes, then whisk until smooth.

3 Place 2 cups of the flour in a large bowl. Stir in the baking powder, baking soda, and salt.

4 Stir the eggs and vanilla into the chocolate mixture. Add the chocolate mixture to the flour mixture, and whisk until smooth. Spoon the batter into the prepared pans, filling them two-thirds full.

5 Bake until the tops are set, about 10 minutes.

6 Meanwhile, combine the fine graham cracker crumbs, large graham cracker chunks, light brown sugar, melted butter, and remaining 2 tablespoons flour in a medium bowl. Sprinkle evenly over the cupcakes, and bake for 7 more minutes.

7 Distribute the marshmallows evenly over the tops of the cupcakes, and bake until the marshmallows are lightly golden, about 5 minutes. Remove from the oven, and cool the pans on wire racks for 5 minutes. Remove the cupcakes from the pans to wire racks, and top each with a milk chocolate candy bar piece. Cool completely, about 30 minutes.

Perfect Yellow Cupcakes with Vanilla Buttercream

Photograph on page 230

There is nothing more classic than a perfect yellow cupcake with vanilla buttercream and rainbow sprinkles. It is a timeless dessert, and therefore one you should have a go-to recipe for. Well, here you go—You're welcome. The ingredients are simple, readily available and it only takes about 20 minutes to whip them together. Say goodbye to those boxed mixes FOREVER (okay that's slightly dramatic, at least save them for a lazy day). These cupcakes are perfectly moist with a beautiful golden hue (thanks, butter and eggs) and the sweet, creamy buttercream is the icing on the cake. Literally. And if you're my kids, you will eat all the frosting first and then attack the rest.

1   Preheat the oven to 350°F. Beat the butter in a stand mixer on medium speed until creamy, about 1 minute. Gradually add the sugar, and beat until light and fluffy, 1 to 2 minutes. Add the eggs, 1 at a time, beating well after each addition.

2   Stir together the flour, baking powder, and salt. Add to the butter mixture alternately with the milk, beginning and ending with the flour mixture. Beat until blended after each addition. Stir in the vanilla.

3   Line 2 (12-cup) standard-sized muffin pans with paper baking cups, and lightly coat with cooking spray. Spoon the batter into the prepared pans, filling two-thirds full.

4   Bake until a wooden pick inserted in the center comes out clean, 15 to 20 minutes. Cool the pans on wire racks for 5 minutes. Remove the cupcakes from the pans to wire racks, and cool completely, about 30 minutes.

5   Meanwhile, Make the Vanilla Buttercream: Beat the butter with an electric mixer on medium speed until creamy, about 1 minute. Gradually add the vanilla, salt, and 1 cup of the powdered sugar, and beat on low speed until combined. Gradually add the remaining powdered sugar alternately with the cream, beating on low speed until blended after each addition. Beat on high speed until light and fluffy, 1 to 2 minutes. Pipe or spread the Vanilla Buttercream over the cupcakes. If desired, top with candy sprinkles.

SERVES **24**
HANDS-ON TIME: **20 MINUTES**
TOTAL TIME: **1 HOUR 10 MINUTES**

1 cup unsalted butter, softened

2 cups granulated sugar

4 large eggs

3 cups sifted all-purpose flour

1 tablespoon baking powder

½ teaspoon table salt

1½ cups whole milk

1 teaspoon vanilla extract

VANILLA BUTTERCREAM

1 cup unsalted butter, softened

1 teaspoon vanilla extract

¼ teaspoon table salt

1 (2-pound) package powdered sugar

¾ cup heavy cream

Rainbow candy sprinkles (optional)

SIRIOUSLY MINI

For a fun variation, stir ½ cup rainbow candy sprinkles into the batter before baking.

SIRIOUSLY FANCY

This batter can be turned into a delicious 2-layer cake. Bake in 2 (9-inch) greased and floured round pans for 30 minutes.

Perfect Yellow
Cupcakes
with Vanilla
Buttercream
PG 229

S'more
Cupcakes
PG 228

Angel Food Cake with Vanilla Strawberries

SERVES **16**
HANDS-ON TIME: **20 MINUTES**
TOTAL TIME: **3 HOURS**

Cake for breakfast is a thing, in case you didn't know, and one of the best kinds to eat in the morning is angel food cake. It's light, delicate and sponge-like, making it an ideal vehicle for loads of fresh fruit. Fruit=breakfast, therefore this cake=breakfast. It's simple math! This recipe calls for strawberries that marinate in sweet sugar and flavorful vanilla bean paste—there's your fruit! The first time I made angel food cake, I was so proud of myself. Yes, it does require a lot of egg whites, but you can use the leftover yolks in shortbread, Hollandaise sauce or pudding. Or scramble them and eat them for breakfast with your cake.

1   Preheat the oven to 350°F. Process the sugar, flour, and salt in a food processor until the mixture is thoroughly combined and the sugar is finely ground, about 1 minute. Set aside.

2   Beat the egg whites in a stand mixer fitted with a whisk attachment on medium speed until foamy, about 1 minute. Add the vanilla bean paste, lemon juice, and cream of tartar, and beat until incorporated. Increase the speed to medium-high, and beat until stiff peaks form, 2 to 3 minutes. Gently fold in the sugar mixture, ⅓ cup at a time, folding just until blended after each addition. Spread the batter evenly in an ungreased 10-inch tube pan (make sure the opening in the tube is large enough to fit over a long-neck bottle) or angel food cake pan.

3   Bake until a wooden pick inserted into the center comes out clean, 38 to 40 minutes. Invert the pan over a wide-based, long-neck glass bottle, fitting the tube over the neck. (This will keep the cake from deflating as it cools.) Cool completely, about 2 hours.

4   Meanwhile, Make the Vanilla Bean Whipped Cream and Vanilla Strawberries: Beat the heavy cream with an electric mixer on medium speed until foamy. With the mixer running, gradually add the granulated sugar and vanilla bean paste. Increase the speed to medium-high, and beat until medium peaks form, 1 to 2 minutes. Chill until ready to serve.

5   For the Vanilla Strawberries, stir together the fresh strawberries, granulated sugar, and vanilla bean paste. Let stand at least 15 minutes, then chill until ready to serve.

6   Loosen the cake from the sides of the pan using a narrow metal spatula, and invert the cake onto a platter. Top with the Vanilla Bean Whipped Cream and serve with the Vanilla Strawberries sprinkled with some fresh mint leaves, if you like.

2 cups granulated sugar

1 cup all-purpose flour

¼ teaspoon table salt

1 ½ cups egg whites, at room temperature (from 13 large eggs)

2 teaspoons vanilla bean paste

1 ½ teaspoons fresh lemon juice

1 teaspoon cream of tartar

VANILLA BEAN WHIPPED CREAM

1 ½ cups heavy cream

3 tablespoons granulated sugar

1 teaspoon vanilla bean paste

VANILLA STRAWBERRIES

1 quart fresh strawberries, quartered

2 tablespoons granulated sugar

1 teaspoon vanilla bean paste

Fresh mint leaves

SIRIOUSLY **FANCY**

Use leftover angel food cake in a homemade trifle...fancy!

SIRIOUSLY **IMPORTANT**

When inverting onto a glass bottle, do so quickly, and onto one with a large base and skinny neck. The large base will help hold the cake up and prevent it from sinking and becoming wet, spongy and sticky. Think: brandy bottle, etc.

Vegetable shortening

2 (4-ounce) bittersweet chocolate baking bars, chopped

½ cup unsalted butter, softened

1 cup granulated sugar

1 cup packed light brown sugar

3 large eggs

2 cups all-purpose flour

1 teaspoon baking soda

½ teaspoon table salt

1 (8-ounce) container sour cream

2 teaspoons vanilla extract

1 cup hot brewed coffee

MOCHA BUTTERCREAM FILLING

2 ½ cups powdered sugar

⅔ cup unsalted butter, softened

1 tablespoon unsweetened cocoa

¼ cup heavy cream

2 teaspoons instant coffee granules

1 teaspoon vanilla extract

CHUNKY FUDGE FROSTING

1 cup unsalted butter, softened

6 cups powdered sugar

⅓ cup unsweetened cocoa

⅓ cup whole milk

1 teaspoon vanilla extract

⅛ teaspoon table salt

1 (4-ounce) bittersweet chocolate baking bar, chopped

Chocolate Dream Layer Cake

This cake is my jam, sans jam. I don't like jam cakes. No offense, Jam. Let's start over...what I'm trying to say is I am all about a chocolate lover's cake and this, my friends, is that and more. For starters, there are three layers of cake that are tender, moist and deeply rich in flavor. In between each is a mocha buttercream filling that is intensely satisfying. Coffee is an excellent way to amplify the chocolate experience in a recipe. Finally, the cake is spread with a chunky chocolate frosting that perfectly completes it. If you dream about chocolate as I do, then this cake is well worth the extra effort that goes into the process. Once it is all said and done, you are left with a sublime masterpiece that is best served with a large glass of cold milk.

1   Preheat the oven to 350°F. Lightly spray 3 (9-inch) round cake pans with cooking spray. Line the bottoms of the pans with parchment paper. Grease (with shortening) and flour the parchment paper and pans.

2   Place the chocolate in a microwavable bowl, and microwave on HIGH until melted and smooth, about 1 minute and 30 seconds, stirring at 30-second intervals.

3   Beat the butter in a stand mixer on medium speed until smooth. Gradually add the sugars, and beat until well incorporated, about 3 minutes. Add the eggs, 1 at a time, beating just until blended after each addition. Add the melted chocolate, beating just until blended.

4   Stir together the flour, baking soda, and salt. Gradually add to the chocolate mixture alternately with the sour cream, beginning and ending with the flour mixture. Beat on low speed just until blended after each addition. (The mixture will be thick.)

5   Stir the vanilla into the hot coffee. Gradually add the coffee mixture to the batter in a slow, steady stream, beating at low speed just until blended. Divide the batter evenly among the prepared pans.

6   Bake until a wooden pick inserted in the center comes out clean, about 24 minutes. Cool in the pans on a wire rack for 10 minutes. Remove from the pans to the wire rack, and cool completely, about 1 hour.

SIRIOUSLY **SIMPLE**

Swap out the chopped chocolate in the Chunky Fudge Frosting layer with chocolate chips, my go-to pantry item.

7   Meanwhile, Make the Mocha Buttercream Filling: Beat the powdered sugar, butter, and cocoa with an electric mixer on medium speed until fluffy, about 3 minutes. Place the cream in a microwavable bowl, and microwave on MEDIUM (50% power) until warm (do not boil), about 45 seconds. Stir together the warm cream and the coffee granules until dissolved; cool for about 5 minutes. Gradually add the cream mixture and vanilla to the butter mixture, and beat on medium speed until smooth, about 2 minutes.

8   Meanwhile, Make the Chunky Fudge Frosting: Beat the butter with an electric mixer on medium speed until creamy. Stir together the powdered sugar and unsweetened cocoa in a medium bowl. Gradually add the cocoa mixture alternately with the milk, beating on medium speed until smooth after each addition. Beat in the vanilla and salt. Stir in the chopped chocolate.

9   Place 1 layer on a serving plate, and spread half of the Mocha Buttercream Filling on the layer. Top with a second layer, and spread the remaining filling on that. Top with the third layer, and spread the top and sides of the cake with the Chunky Fudge Frosting.

Coconut Bundt Cake with Coconut Milk Glaze

SERVES 16
HANDS-ON TIME: 20 MINUTES
TOTAL TIME: 4 HOURS

I love Bundt cakes—even though in all honesty, I don't know how to pronounce "Bundt"—because they look so professional. Anything that effortlessly comes out of the oven in a cylindrical shape with beautiful ridged edges is a winner in my book. And this is my book! This Bundt cake is rich like a pound cake, yet moist and tender at the same time, with a tropical flair. The nuttiness of the pecans brings out even more of the coconut flavor, and the glaze adds one more element of the tropics to the finished product. The only thing difficult about this recipe is waiting for it to bake and cool, because the aromas filling your kitchen will be irresistible. Your patience will pay off, however, because flipping the pan without the use of oven mitts will ensure the cake holds its alluring shape. Now, someone please teach me how to say "Bundt."

1 Preheat the oven to 325°F. Beat the butter and cream cheese in a stand mixer on medium speed until creamy, 2 to 3 minutes. Gradually add the sugar, beating on medium speed until light and fluffy, about 4 to 6 minutes. Add the eggs, 1 at a time, beating just until the yellow disappears after each addition.

2 Stir together the flour and salt; add to the butter mixture alternately with the coconut milk, beginning and ending with the flour. Beat on low speed just until blended after each addition. Stir in the vanilla extract, coconut extract, pecans, and coconut. Pour the batter into a well-greased (with shortening) and floured 15-cup Bundt pan.

3 Bake until a long wooden pick inserted in the center comes out clean, 1 hour and 20 minutes to 1 hour and 30 minutes. Cool in the pan on a wire rack for 20 minutes. Remove from the pan to a wire rack, and cool completely, about 2 hours.

4 When the cake is cooled, Make the Coconut Glaze: Whisk together all the ingredients in a small bowl. Immediately spoon the Coconut Glaze over the cake, and, if desired, garnish with toasted coconut and chopped toasted pecans.

1 ½ cups unsalted butter, softened

1 (8-ounce) package cream cheese, softened

3 cups granulated sugar

6 large eggs

3 cups all-purpose flour

½ teaspoon table salt

¼ cup well-shaken and stirred coconut milk

1 teaspoon vanilla extract

½ teaspoon coconut extract

1 cup chopped toasted pecans

½ cup sweetened shredded coconut

Vegetable shortening

COCONUT GLAZE

2 cups powdered sugar

3 tablespoons well-shaken and stirred coconut milk

1 teaspoon vanilla extract

Toasted sweetened shredded coconut and chopped toasted pecans, for garnish (optional)

SERVES **8**

HANDS-ON TIME: **20 MINUTES**

TOTAL TIME: **3 HOURS**

1 (16-ounce) package peanut butter sandwich cookies (such as Nutter Butter), plus a few crushed for garnish

½ cup lightly salted dry-roasted peanuts

½ cup unsalted butter, melted

1 (8-ounce) package cream cheese, softened

1 cup packed light brown sugar

¾ cup creamy peanut butter

1 cup heavy cream

2 teaspoons vanilla extract

2 medium bananas

VANILLA WHIPPED CREAM TOPPING

1 cup heavy cream

½ teaspoon vanilla extract

3 tablespoons powdered sugar

Chopped lightly salted dry-roasted peanuts, for garnish

SIRIOUSLY SIMPLE

You can make the crust the night before and let it cool so it's ready to go in the morning when you make your filling.

Peanut Butter–Banana Cream Pie

This flavor combination is what my husband dreams about. I know that for a fact, because sometimes he talks in his sleep and says things like, "Nutter Butter crust…peanut butter filling…whipped cream topping…bananas." It's weird. However, after you taste this pie you will understand that it is what dreams are made of. Let's start with the crust, made from peanut butter cookie sandwiches, salty peanuts and melted butter…it supplies the perfect crunchy vessel for your filling and carries the peanut butter flavor throughout the pie. Then the filling, which features creamy peanut butter and cream cheese, is light, airy and a wonderful contrast to the sliced bananas and crunchy crust. The pie is dolloped with a vanilla whipped topping and chopped peanuts for a beautiful finish that won't last long, because you will want to dive right in. Sweet dreams!

1 Preheat the oven to 350°F. Process the cookies and peanuts in a food processor until finely chopped, about 1 minute. Stir together the cookie mixture and melted butter. Press the crumb mixture on the bottom, up the sides, and onto the lip of a lightly greased 9-inch pie plate.

2 Bake until lightly browned, 10 to 12 minutes. Transfer to a wire rack, and cool completely, about 30 minutes.

3 Beat the cream cheese, brown sugar, peanut butter, and 1 tablespoon of the heavy cream with an electric mixer on medium speed until light and fluffy, 2 to 3 minutes.

4 Place the remaining heavy cream in a bowl, and add the vanilla. Beat on medium speed until stiff peaks form, about 2 minutes. Fold one-third of the whipped cream into the peanut butter mixture, then gently fold the remaining whipped cream into the peanut butter mixture.

5 Slice the bananas, and place in an even layer on the crust. Spread the peanut butter mixture evenly over the bananas.

6 Make the Vanilla Whipped Cream Topping: Beat the heavy cream and vanilla with an electric mixer on medium speed until foamy, about 1 minute. Increase the speed to medium-high, and gradually add the powdered sugar, beating until stiff peaks form, about 2 minutes. (Do not overbeat.)

7 Dollop the topping over the peanut butter mixture. Chill for 2 hours. Garnish with the chopped peanuts and crushed cookies, if desired.

Mom's Rhubarb Crisp

Growing up, I wanted nothing to do with this dessert. Rhubarb scared me. It's not technically a fruit but it's prepared like one, it looks like red celery and then there's the name...rhubarb. I mean, more kid-friendly names exist in this world. However, had I tried my mother's recipe back then, I would have discovered that tangy rhubarb and sweet strawberries make the best of friends in this yummy, cobbler-style crisp. The stalky, leafy plant is in season during the springtime—my mom always grew it in her garden—but if you don't have fresh rhubarb on hand you can use frozen. Once it is gently processed in the thick sauce, it softens without falling apart, and along with the berries creates a sweet mixture. It is then sandwiched in between a sugary crumble and baked until bubbly and golden. Topped with vanilla ice cream, it's the perfect dessert.

1   Preheat the oven to 350°F. Combine the brown sugar, flour, oats, butter, nuts, and cinnamon in a bowl until crumbly. Press half of the brown sugar mixture onto the bottom of an 8-inch square pan. (It's not necessary to grease the pan.)

2   Stir together the granulated sugar, water, cornstarch, and vanilla in a saucepan over medium-high, and cook, stirring often, until very thick. Remove from the heat.

3   Add the rhubarb and strawberries, and stir until thoroughly combined. Spread over the crumble in the pan. Top with the remaining half of the brown sugar mixture.

4   Bake until browned and bubbly, about 1 hour. Serve warm with vanilla ice cream.

SERVES **8**

HANDS-ON TIME: **20 MINUTES**

TOTAL TIME: **1 HOUR 20 MINUTES**

1 cup packed light brown sugar

1 cup all-purpose flour

¾ cup uncooked old-fashioned regular rolled oats

½ cup unsalted butter, melted

½ cup chopped walnuts or pecans

1 teaspoon ground cinnamon

1 cup granulated sugar

1 cup water

3 tablespoons cornstarch

1 teaspoon vanilla extract

1 ½ pounds rhubarb, trimmed and cut into ½-inch-thick slices

8 ounces fresh strawberries, hulled and chopped

Vanilla ice cream, for serving

SIRIOUSLY **VARIED**

You can easily swap out the strawberries for fresh blueberries.

1 (14.1-ounce) package refrigerated piecrusts

10 (3 ½-inch) canning jar lids and rings

5 Granny Smith apples, peeled and chopped

¼ cup granulated sugar

1 tablespoon fresh lemon juice

1 teaspoon ground cinnamon

¼ teaspoon ground nutmeg

¼ teaspoon table salt

2 tablespoons unsalted butter, melted

SALTED CARAMEL SAUCE

1 cup heavy cream

1 ½ cups packed light brown sugar

¼ cup unsalted butter

1 tablespoon vanilla extract

½ teaspoon table salt

Vanilla ice cream, for serving

SIRIOUSLY **SIMPLE**

Leftover caramel sauce can be stored, covered, in the refrigerator up to 1 week. This would be delicious on ice cream, pound cake, or fresh fruit. Simply reheat in the microwave on HIGH for 30 seconds to 1 minute.

Mini Apple Tarts with Salted Caramel Sauce

I truly enjoy anything miniature-sized. I steal tiny condiments from hotels, I adore teeny little bowls and spoons, don't even get me started about all the "tiny home" shows on TV...basically anything super small makes me feel like a giant and that is fun. But let's talk about food. These Mini Apple Tarts are the absolute cutest desserts because they are baked in mason jar lids! Adorable! Unique! Also brilliant, because the jar lids with removable bottoms mimic actual tart pans. These are classically delicious due to the juicy, tart apples with hints of warm cinnamon and nutmeg. They are not overly sweet, so the salted caramel sauce provides the perfect touch and gives them a modern twist (which, by the way, is great to make on its own to drizzle over ice cream or brownies). How fun would these be at a summer cookout or a back-to-school picnic? Mini perfection in a jar...lid.

1   Preheat the oven to 375°F. Roll out 1 piecrust to a 13-inch circle on a lightly floured surface; cut 5 circles using a 4 ½-inch round cutter. Repeat with the remaining piecrust. Place the jar rings on a baking sheet, and place the lids inside with the rubber seal facing down. Lightly grease each lid and ring with cooking spray. Place 1 cutout piecrust circle in each prepared jar lid, and gently flute the top.

2   Place the apples, granulated sugar, lemon juice, cinnamon, nutmeg, and salt in a medium bowl, and stir to combine. Gently stir in the melted butter. Place about ½ cup of the mixture in each prepared pie shell.

3   Bake until the crust is golden brown, 35 to 40 minutes. Cool in the pans on a wire rack for 20 minutes, then gently lift out of rings. Serve warm, or cool completely.

4   Meanwhile, Make the Salted Caramel Sauce: Bring the cream to a light boil in a large saucepan over medium heat, stirring occasionally. Add the brown sugar, and cook, stirring often, until dissolved and the mixture is smooth, 4 to 5 minutes. Remove from the heat, and stir in the butter, vanilla, and salt. Cool for 10 minutes, and serve warm alongside the tarts and vanilla ice cream.

Blueberry Skillet Cobbler

When I graduated college, I moved from Wisconsin to California for a job on the TV show *Frasier*. It was the final season of the highly esteemed and awarded series, thus my very first experience as a production assistant completely spoiled me. We were fed, practically every meal, from the best restaurants in Los Angeles (even though it fell on me to place the giant order and pick up the food). It was during this (indulgent) time that I fell in love with blueberry cobbler, and I knew one day I would have to create my own version. In this recipe, everything is easily prepared and then baked in a heavy, cast-iron skillet, which is visually appealing and easy to maneuver. The blueberry mixture is rich, juicy and bright thanks to the zest of lemon, and the cobbler is moist and cake-y. Everything comes together beautifully in this bubbly dessert that is best accompanied with a scoop of ice cream and a cup of coffee.

SERVES **12**
HANDS-ON TIME: **20 MINUTES**
TOTAL TIME: **1 HOUR 40 MINUTES**

3 tablespoons cornstarch

1 tablespoon lemon zest

1 ½ cups packed light brown sugar

1 ¾ pounds fresh blueberries

Vegetable shortening

½ cup unsalted butter, softened

2 large eggs

1 ½ cups all-purpose flour

1 ½ teaspoons baking powder

¼ teaspoon table salt

1 (8-ounce) container sour cream

½ teaspoon baking soda

Vanilla ice cream, for serving

1 Preheat the oven to 350°F. Stir together the cornstarch, lemon zest, and ½ cup of the brown sugar in a large bowl. Toss the blueberries with the cornstarch mixture, and spoon into a greased (with shortening) 10-inch cast-iron skillet.

2 Beat the butter in a stand mixer on medium speed until fluffy, about 1 minute. Gradually add the remaining 1 cup brown sugar, beating until light and fluffy, about 2 minutes. Add the eggs, 1 at a time, beating just until blended after each addition.

3 Stir together the flour, baking powder, and salt in a small bowl. Stir together the sour cream and baking soda in a separate bowl. Add the flour mixture to the butter mixture alternately with the sour cream mixture, beginning and ending with the flour mixture. Beat on low speed just until blended after each addition. Spoon the batter over the blueberry mixture in the skillet.

4 Bake until the batter topping just begins to brown, 33 to 35 minutes. Cover loosely with aluminum foil (to prevent excessive browning), and bake until a wooden pick inserted in the center of the topping comes out clean, 16 to 18 more minutes. Let stand for at least 30 minutes, and serve warm with vanilla ice cream.

SIRIOUSLY IMPORTANT

Be patient and let this sit for the full 30 minutes it calls for, because this allows everything to set and hold together.

SIRIOUSLY VARIED

You can easily swap whole-fat Greek yogurt for the sour cream.

BLUE LAYER

1 cup fresh blueberries

1 cup vanilla whole-milk yogurt

1 tablespoon honey

1 teaspoon fresh lemon juice

GREEN LAYER

1 small ripe banana, sliced

1 cup baby spinach

1 cup vanilla whole-milk yogurt

1 tablespoon honey

1 teaspoon fresh lemon juice

RED LAYER

1 cup sliced fresh strawberries

1 cup vanilla whole-milk yogurt

1 tablespoon honey

1 teaspoon fresh lemon juice

ORANGE LAYER

1 cup chopped fresh peaches

1 cup vanilla whole-milk yogurt

1 tablespoon honey

1 teaspoon fresh lemon juice

Rainbow Popsicles

If I know one thing, it is that kids love rainbows and kids love popsicles. That is more than one thing, but I can't help it because I know so much. I'm sure you are also aware that all of us—kids and grownups alike—first eat with our eyes, so anything that is visually appealing is hard to pass up. I had seen versions of these beautiful creations on the Internet, and I was so excited to try out my own recipe. To make them, you start by blending various combinations of fruits and veggies with yogurt, honey and lemon juice. For the colors you use strawberries for red, peaches for orange, spinach for green (and I promise, you barely taste the vegetable here) and blueberries for blue. Each layer is distinctly flavorful, and the creamy yogurt base keeps them from melting too quickly. Once poured into the molds, everything swirls together to develop a lovely rainbow of colors that is as nutritious as it is delicious.

Process each layer separately in a high-powered blender until smooth. Pour the mixtures into 3-ounce ice pop molds, alternating the colors. Top with a lid, and insert craft sticks. Freeze for 8 to 12 hours.

SIRIOUSLY **IMPORTANT**

When pouring the mixtures in the popsicle molds, it's helpful to think about which mixtures are thicker than others. Alternate thick and thin mixtures so that they don't blend colors too much. Also, stir the blueberry mixture before pouring into the molds. The pectin will start to make it gel a little if it sits too long.

SIRIOUSLY **SIMPLE**

If you don't want to make 22 popsicles, swirl the leftover mixture in a glass and drink it as a smoothie or prepare it as a smoothie bowl.

Metric Equivalents

COOKING/OVEN TEMPERATURES

	Fahrenheit	Celsius	Gas Mark
Freeze Water	32° F	0° C	
Room Temp.	68° F	20° C	
Boil Water	212° F	100° C	
Bake	325° F	160° C	3
	350° F	180° C	4
	375° F	190° C	5
	400° F	200° C	6
	425° F	220° C	7
	450° F	230° C	8
Broil			Grill

LIQUID INGREDIENTS BY VOLUME

¼ tsp					=	1 ml		
½ tsp					=	2 ml		
1 tsp					=	5 ml		
3 tsp	=	1 Tbsp	=	½ fl oz	=	15 ml		
2 Tbsp	=	⅛ cup	=	1 fl oz	=	30 ml		
4 Tbsp	=	¼ cup	=	2 fl oz	=	60 ml		
5 ⅓ Tbsp	=	⅓ cup	=	3 fl oz	=	80 ml		
8 Tbsp	=	½ cup	=	4 fl oz	=	120 ml		
10 ⅔ Tbsp	=	⅔ cup	=	5 fl oz	=	160 ml		
12 Tbsp	=	¾ cup	=	6 fl oz	=	180 ml		
16 Tbsp	=	1 cup	=	8 fl oz	=	240 ml		
1 pt	=	2 cups	=	16 fl oz	=	480 ml		
1 qt	=	4 cups	=	32 fl oz	=	960 ml		
				33 fl oz	=	1000 ml	=	1 l

DRY INGREDIENTS BY WEIGHT

(To convert ounces to grams, multiply the number of ounces by 30.)

1 oz	=	¹⁄₁₆ lb	=	30 g
4 oz	=	¼ lb	=	120 g
8 oz	=	½ lb	=	240 g
12 oz	=	¾ lb	=	360 g
16 oz	=	1 lb	=	480 g

LENGTH

(To convert inches to centimeters, multiply inches by 2.5.)

1 in					=	2.5 cm		
12 in	=	1 ft			=	30 cm		
36 in	=	3 ft	=	1 yd	=	90 cm		
40 in	=					100 cm	=	1 m

EQUIVALENTS FOR DIFFERENT TYPES OF INGREDIENTS

Standard Cup	Fine Powder (ex. flour)	Grain (ex. rice)	Granular (ex. sugar)	Liquid Solids (ex. butter)	Liquid (ex. milk)
1	140 g	150 g	190 g	200 g	240 ml
¾	105 g	113 g	143 g	150 g	180 ml
⅔	93 g	100 g	125 g	133 g	160 ml
½	70 g	75 g	95 g	100 g	120 ml
⅓	47 g	50 g	63 g	67 g	80 ml
¼	35 g	38 g	48 g	50 g	60 ml
⅛	18 g	19 g	24 g	25 g	30 ml

Acknowledgments

To my brilliant cookbook editor, Anja Schmidt. Thank you for holding my hand through this foreign process and for understanding when life got tough and extensions were needed. You=the best.

To the incomparable Ellen Silverman, photographer extraordinaire, who makes standing on top of an island with a camera look effortless. Thank you for beautifully capturing my chaotic kitchen.

Thanks to the talented crew of recipe developers, testers, photographers and stylists down in Birmingham's Time Inc. Food Studios.

To Allison Chi and Matt Ryan for making my book look the way I always dreamt it would.

To so many others at Time Inc., including Melissa Brown, Paden Reich, Greg Amason, Mary Ann Laurens, Jacqueline Giovanelli and Dolores Hydock... I humbly thank you all. And to the PR and marketing team, Danielle Costa, Amanda Lipnick and Kourtney Sokmen...thank you for helping me sell this thing!

To the team at Dixon Talent: James "Babydoll" Dixon, Dan Bodansky and Ben Taren. Thank you for your guidance and unwavering support.

To the Clutterbucks: Thank you for generously offering your home up, even though you had just moved and discovered you were pregnant with your third child. Canadians > Americans.

To Savannah Guthrie for writing my Foreword: Thank you for your kind friendship and interest in browning butter. And to the support of Catherine McCord, Jenna Bush Hager and Jimmy Kimmel...you are all super human beings.

To the unshakable Laurie Brandt, who can do ANYTHING: You are our rock.

To our fantastic nanny Priscilla (or "YaYa" as the kids call her)...Thank you for giving me the greatest gift: TIME, and for fiercely loving and protecting my children.

To so many friends: my Real Moms In Grey, my Congo Moms (because we live in a jungle?), my Cali Breakfast Club, the Manhasset Boat Crew...all of you know who you are, and I value your friendship like I value air.

To my family. ALL OF YOU. Your support means everything.

To Kiki and Pops, our guardian angels: I miss you every day, and I feel your love deep in my bones.

To my children, Jackson, Etta and London: You are my greatest accomplishment, nothing else compares. Thank you for putting up with Mommy always working at her computer or in the kitchen. I hope one day you'll eat broccoli.

To my husband, Bingo (I married a clown): Thank you for being in my corner. I love you. Bloggity bloggity.

And finally, to YOU! There would be no book without you. Thank you!

Index

C